D0499844

Between Two Worlds

BETWEEN
TWO WORLDS

VOLUME I

TORN BETWEEN:

The World I Know and Love

and

The World I Love and Don't Know

SAM RADOBENKO

XULON PRESS ELITE

Xulon Press Elite
2301 Lucien Way #415
Maitland, FL 32751
407.339.4217
www.xulonpress.com

© 2020 by Sam Radobenko

All rights reserved solely by the author. The author guarantees all contents are original and do not infringe upon the legal rights of any other person or work. No part of this book may be reproduced in any form without the permission of the author. The views expressed in this book are not necessarily those of the publisher.

Printed in the United States of America.

ISBN-13: 978-1-6305-0842-5

TABLE OF CONTENTS

INTRODUCTION

I've read the Book of Enoch, an ancient text referred to in the Bible, Jude, chapter one. According to Enoch, during his life he traveled from earth to Heaven a total of eight times. During his seventh trip to Heaven, he was told by God that he would be going back to earth only one more time, and that he would be staying on the earth for only thirty days. This way he could enjoy his family and inform them of his pending final journey. After completion of the thirty days, he would be returning to Heaven for his final trip home. What he writes about encountering on each trip is not only informative but utterly amazing.

I've also read a book written by an author who, to my knowledge, is still alive today. In his book, he recounts a four-hour trip he took to Heaven one Sunday afternoon. I've watched him as he just beams while sharing his amazing story.

And I've read the book 40 Days in Heaven: The True Testimony of Seneca Sodi's Visitation to Paradise, the Holy City and the Glory of God's Throne. This wonderful book, written by Reverend Elwood Scott, is so mind blowing, it just makes one's head spin. Imagine being in Heaven for forty consecutive days and then being sent back to earth so you could tell about what you'd seen, heard, and witnessed. Wow, where would you start?

So one day, while I was reflecting on all of the above, I thought, "Well, why not me?" After all, God says in His Word that we can ask Him for anything, right? So why couldn't I, at the age of sixty-six, ask God to keep my body alive but let my spirit travel to my future home for a sneak visit from time to time? I could learn about that home and have a one-on-one, face-to-face encounter with the Son of God. I could visit with friends, loved ones, and patriarch's that have gone before. Then I could come back and share what I've seen, heard, and learned with those still here on earth that might be slightly interested. That sounds crazy doesn't it?

Well, that's exactly what I did. As of the writing of this book, I've taken fifty trips. But I don't want to get ahead of myself. I want to share with you those events that led up to my first journey, then the second, the third, etc. I know there will be more. I'm already eagerly looking forward to the next and to those beyond that. This will be an ongoing process for me.

So one day, while I was having a conversation with our Heavenly Father, I asked Him. Since others have obviously gone there and returned, could I?

His answer surprised me. Yes, but only when He felt the time was right. In other words, I would not know when the right time was or where I would be or what I would be doing. It would just happen.

Now I realize this may sound too good to be true, that some who read what's in the following pages won't believe it. Some might say what I have is a very vivid imagination but that it simply didn't happen. However, in spite of the sceptics, there will be those who will see the truth in my words. My job is not to convince you that what I've encountered is real, but simply to experience it and then write down those experiences so that you may be encouraged by what you read, for Heaven is very real, and many of our loved ones, friends, and patriarchs from the past are very much alive today. I've been there and met many of them. So my challenge to you is that as you read this book, you allow the Holy Spirit to guide you so that you will enjoy the journey. I certainly did, and I look forward to many more.

This, then, is my journey—from the beginning.

THE JOURNEYS

Journey Number 1

PLANETS, STARS & GALAXIES

It was Sunday, September 17, 2017. I can't remember whether it was the previous Wednesday or Thursday evening. I had exercised hard that Wednesday, and then worked just as hard on the backyard Thursday morning. Anyway, it was bedtime now on Thursday, and as I crawled into bed, the Lord spoke to me. "Are you ready?" He said. "Get out of bed and get on your knees."

"Now?" I said. "I'm so exhausted. Can't we do it some other time?"

"OK," He said, and soon I was fast asleep.

Sunday morning, just a few hours later, I got up and headed for the shower. Standing in the shower, lukewarm water running down my back, I heard His voice again. "Are you ready?"

I was startled but said yes. I was facing the corner of the shower, away from the running water, and placed both my forearms against the walls. Then it happened—swoosh, I was gone. Not my body, but my inner body, my spirit body. I was outside of my physical body, and I was traveling very fast. I was not in any type of vehicle. There were no angels or horses of any kind, just me.

All I could see was a vast array of planets and stars, an incredible and unbelievable sight. My first thought was that I wasn't traveling so fast that all I could see were colors zooming by me in a blur. Everything was very clear. My attention was drawn to all the planets and stars, and I wasn't traveling toward the sun. If the sun

1

was straight ahead of you, I was traveling upward, away from it. Everywhere I looked, I saw stars, planets, etc. The view was just breathtaking. Clusters of stars were near me, others farther away. They were everywhere. Simply put, the view was breathtaking. Words can't adequately describe the view. Then they were not far away, because I was in or among them. They were all around me. Different colors appeared in them—reds, blues, emerald greens, etc. There were all so beautiful to gaze at. I was just speechless.

All of a sudden, I was there. I didn't see it ahead of time. I was just there. However, I wasn't inside of Heaven, but outside. It must have been Paradise. It was just beautiful.

There were breathtaking green trees, grass, and substantial mountains in the distance. I didn't notice the sky, or whether the sun was shining, or even if there was a sky. I didn't take time to see if there were any people either.

As I was staring at what I was seeing, it must have been time to leave, because now I was traveling back, I assume toward the earth. Once again the stars. I was again consumed by them. They were all around me, then farther and farther away. I could now see the earth. Wow, what a wonderful sight it was, now getting bigger and bigger, with its colors filling my view. Then, I was back standing in my shower. "What just happened?" I wondered. Then He spoke to me a second time.

Journey Number 2

Seeing Heaven for the First Time

I don't know how long I was gone the first time. Seconds, minute? I just don't know. But I heard Him say, "Do you want to go again?"

Still standing in the shower, I answered yes, and before I knew it, swoosh, I was gone again. However, this time I was riding in what appeared to be some type of cart or chariot. There were no horses or angels operating this thing. It just went by itself. And I wasn't standing; I was sitting down. I don't know how long the journey there took the second time. All I know is that I was traveling very fast, but it wasn't so fast that I couldn't take in the scenery. I was once again caught up in all of the amazing beauty of the vast array of stars and planets. As I turned my head slightly to the left, I could see the sun. I didn't feel the heat from it, and I must have been pulling away from it because it appeared to be getting smaller and smaller.

Then I was there again, just outside of Heaven. I don't know how I knew, but I knew this place was Paradise. I stepped out of the cart or chariot and looked around this time. I saw a great wall. It was so large I couldn't see the top of it. It just went on and on—farther than I could see. Looking first to my right and then to the left, I simply couldn't see the end of it. But the colors were just amazing.

At the base, it looked like about a dozen different colors that went on and on for as far as I was able to see. Some of the colors I wasn't sure if I'd ever seen before. The place I was standing in—the beauty is out of the world. Once again, I didn't notice whether anyone else was there, I just don't recall seeing anyone. I can't tell you just how long I was standing and just looking; however, I soon knew it was time to go. I don't recall climbing back into the cart or chariot, but now I was traveling in reverse order again. I was caught up again in the beauty of the galaxy and the cosmos. I don't recall approaching the earth this time, but soon I found myself once again in the shower, not sure just how long I'd been gone.

It was difficult finishing my shower. I feel like I was in a daze. Did what I think happened really happen, or was it just my imagination? My head felt like I was in a cloud. After my shower, I dressed, went into the living room, and sat in my favorite easy chair, still completely dazed. About five minutes went by, and then I heard His voice. "I have so much more to show you. I give you permission to call the traveling angel anytime that you want. You do not have to wait on me." Then He was gone. I wanted to talk to Him. I had so many questions to ask.

Journey Number 3

FACE-TO-FACE WITH THE
KING OF KINGS

So there I was, sitting in the easy chair. I'd just taken not one but two amazing trips, and I'd heard from the One who made everything. I felt like I couldn't move. I was numb. A few minutes went by as I was recalling all that had just happened. Then it hit me. If I wanted to go back, He said, all I had to do was call the traveling angel. I decide to try it.

The clock said it was 8:22 a.m. "In the name of Jesus," I said. "I call the traveling angel to come and pick me up." Next, I don't know how, but my inner body, my spirit body, left my physical body and went out the front door. In the front yard was a chariot, just hovering, with an angel in the front. I'd never seen a chariot like this before. It was mostly red and had gold engravings or inscriptions. There were no flames and no wheels. The chariot was not enclosed, and it had a couple of seats. I looked at the angel, and he just turned around, looked at me, and smiled. Then we were off. The ride was spectacular, just like before. In what seemed to be a twinkling of an eye, there we are again, away from the earth and looking at the galaxy. Then we were in the midst of the stars again. The stars glistened, almost as though they were trying to speak to me, or to someone. What an awesome sight.

Now we were back in Paradise. This time, the chariot stopped, and I got out. I didn't see it leave, because I was caught up in the sights of Paradise. I wasn't sure if I saw the great wall this time, because as I was trying to take in the beauty of Paradise. I heard a voice to my left. As I turned, there He was—Jesus, the King of Kings!

I've often thought, "When it's your time for me to leave this earth, who would I like to see? Jesus, my dad, my brother, in-laws, other relatives, friends, all those that have gone before, or the patriarch's from the Bible?" And I've wondered what I'd do when I saw Jesus, the King of Kings. Would I embrace Him, raise my hands in praise to Him, kneel in reverence to Him, or just fall to the floor because of His awesome presence.

Tears started streaming down my face as I fell to the floor. I couldn't believe He was standing in front of me. Within a few moments, I was standing again, and we were face-to-face. His hair was shoulder length and dark brown. He had a beard but not a full beard. He also had a mustache. I was mesmerized by His eyes.

"I'm so glad you are here," He said. His face shinned so lovingly. I felt such peace with Him. When He looked at me, it was as though He could see right through me, and His smile was so infectious. I wanted to never leave His side. "I've got so much for you to see and do here," He said. "You will be back and forth many times, so you will be able to provide a glimpse to those who are mine still on the earth. Great calamity is coming on the earth, and I want you to tell them all about this place for Me—what you have encountered here. I want them to be encouraged. I am charging you with this assignment. Tell them that I am coming soon, very soon." With that He turned around and was gone.

Then I was back in the chariot, and soon, away we went. I wasn't interested in the stars, because I'd just had an encounter with the King of Kings. Then, once again, I was sitting in my easy chair. I looked at the clock. It was 8:38 a.m. I'd been gone for eighteen minutes.

Journey Number 4

ABRAHAM & THE NEW CITY

O n Tuesday, October 3, 2017, at about two thirty in the afternoon, the house was quiet. Once again, I was sitting in my easy chair, spending some one-on-one time with the Lord. As we finished our conversation, I thought about some of the matters we'd spoken about—things pertaining to me, people on my list, things I wanted to do, some items of His plan, special instructions for me, etc.

Then it was quiet again, and I was thinking it would be a good time to take another trip. "In the name of Jesus I said, "I call for the traveling angel to come and pick me up."

Just like before, my inner body, my spirit body, went out the front door. As before, the angel-driven chariot was waiting in the front yard. Just like before, it had no wheels and was just hovering. As I approached, the angel smiled at me. I wondered what the angel was thinking. We left, and this time the route was different. Before, we were not heading for the sun, but this time, for a few moments, we were. I could feel the heat from the sun. Then he turned north, and we were traveling away from the sun once again. It seemed as though I didn't have as much time as before to embrace the cluster of stars and planets, and I summarized that we must have been traveling faster than before, for before I realize it, we were there. However, we didn't land outside the gates like before. This time, we landed right inside Heaven.

As the chariot came to a stop, and I began to step out, my eyes were not fixed on the beauty of this place, because I saw people everywhere. They weren't just moving about, but many were waving at me, or so it seemed. Just as I was about to raise my right arm and wave back, I heard a voice from behind me.

"Hello," said a man.

I turned around to see who it was, and somehow I knew instantly it was Abraham. He was a burly, barrel-chested man who looked like he was in his early thirties. He had a full beard and heavy mustache.

"I've come to welcome you and show you around," he said.

We shook hands, and I felt we'd known each other for a long time. He was like an old shirt or sweater that feels just so comfortable, and as we talked, that's how he made me feel. The chariot was now gone, and the two of us were just standing there. He pointed out the massive wall surrounding Heaven. I got excited, as I now realized where I was, that I was actually "on the inside." It was bright and sunny, but I didn't see or feel the sun. Furthermore, I had no idea of time, or if time even mattered there.

Just then, someone else called my name from somewhere nearby. "Sam," a man said.

As I turned slightly to my right, I saw him running toward me. Instantly I recognized him as my father-in-law Merle. He'd been there just slightly under a year. As we embraced, he said, "I heard you were coming."

I thought, "How did you know?"

He looked fantastic, for a man who had no front teeth and who was in his mid-nineties when he passed away. Now he looked like he was in his early thirties, and as he smiled at me, I could see that he not only had a full set of teeth, but a full head of dark hair as well. Wow, what a handsome looking man he was. "How are you, and how are my daughters doing?" he asked. "We heard they weren't doing too well there for a while. Are they doing better now? When you see them next, tell them we've been praying for them. Boy, it's really good to see you. There's so much here that I want to tell you about and show you. How long will you be staying?"

"I'm not sure," I said.

Then he started to leave but told me he was going to find Betty, my mother-in-law, to let her know I was there.

First, I was blown away by the thought that saints who'd gone to be with the Lord were praying for those who were still alive on the earth. Also, I wasn't sure if he was referring to himself and my mother-in-law as the only ones that were praying for their daughters, or if he had rallied all of Heaven to pray. It was also interesting to me that it must be different when one lives in Heaven and can see the throne room where all the prayers of the saints end up, as compared to still being on the earth, where the saints on the earth send their prayers up to Heaven. How cool is that. I still couldn't get over the thought that saints in Heaven were praying for those still here on the earth. Wow!

As he was leaving and I was watching him go, I heard another person call my name. Without turning to see who it was, I recognized that voice. It was my dad. And I saw him jogging toward me. He came up to me and we embraced. He looked so good. He didn't look like a man in his eighties, which he was. Now he looked like he was in his early to mid-thirties, with a full head of reddish-blond hair. He also had that infectious smile and the bluest blue eyes. When we embraced, he hugged me like I'd never been hugged by him before. He was strong and vibrant.

"At first, when I heard that you were coming, I thought you were coming to stay permanently because it was your time. Then I was told you were on an assignment from the Father. Praise the Lord, praise the Lord, praise the Lord!" Then Abraham starts to praise the Lord with him, and soon all three of us were worshipping the Lord together. When we finished worshipping, Dad said, "When you see that women I love, tell her I was praying for her."

9

With that, Abraham indicated that we must leave, for he had to show me a few things. Dad said, "Good, we'll talk later," and began to walk away.

I can't remember how we traveled, but now found myself with Abraham, standing in front of one of the openings of New City Jerusalem. It was a massive city within the walls of Heaven, and Abraham encouraged me to take a look inside. As I walked in, I was completely blown away. Everything was made out of the purest white gold—buildings, walls, streets, everything. It looked like it was finished, as far as I could see. I was just in waiting for the appropriate time. I was breathless with its beauty.

Next Abraham took me on a small journey. From a distance of a couple of blocks, he showed me my personal future home. I didn't know why we weren't going closer. Perhaps on another trip.

Then it was time to leave, and once again I was back in the chariot for the return trip. I found myself sitting in my easy chair. I'd been gone just under thirty minutes.

Journey Number 5

GALAXIES AFAR

October 17, 2017. It was late, and I'd turned in for the evening. I was about to fall asleep, when I heard His voice. "Get out of bed, and sit in the chair in your bedroom."

So, now I was sitting in the rocking chair, but I wasn't rocking. I felt like I should be asleep. I didn't remember calling for the traveling angel or the chariot, but now I found myself sitting in the chariot, and off we went. As we traveled, I was looking for familiar sights that I'd seen before—Heavenly landmarks, if you will. I recognized a few: certain planets in our solar system, bundles of stars, the sun, and I was looking for Heaven. But we didn't appear to be going in that direction. We were moving to the left of them. We kept going and going and going. We were so far out there that all I saw were new galaxies. However, we weren't slowing down. If anything, we appeared to be speeding up. Galaxy after galaxy appeared, with no end in sight. I was thinking two things. First, does this ever end, and do we ever get to the end? Second, even though I was in a chariot controlled by one of God's angelic creations, I was beginning to get somewhat concerned that we'd never be able to find our way back.

The angel driving must have been able to read my thoughts. "The pathway we've traveled was clear, so you need not worry about finding our way back. We're guided by the Holy Spirit, for the Spirit of God is everywhere, even out here. It is He who guides our path, both to where we want to go, as well as to where we'll return. You wonder if we will come to the end. Well, there never is or will be an end. All things, including the creation here in space, continue to grow, even the galaxies that the Master has put into place."

Now I was beginning to understand, and with that understanding, I just sat back and enjoyed the view. Before I knew it, I was back sitting in the rocking chair, not sure how long I'd been away, but it must have been quite a while.

Journey Number 6

ANGELS TO THE RESCUE IN THE COLLAPSE

I t was Sunday, October 22, 2017, at twelve thirty a.m. I was just awakened from a dream that I'll never forget. Of all of the books I've read and people I've spoken to about the subject, no one has ever told me that in their dream, they died. However, in my dream, I did. In my dream, I was in a building like a school. This school was hit with a violent earthquake, and the building collapsed over and around me, also trapping many children, teachers, and workers. For a brief moment, I was still alive. My body was folded up as though I was sitting. There was a small pocket of air around me, and I was aware of what had just happened. In just a few seconds, the second tremor hit, the pocket collapsed, and I was crushed. I was killed instantly. That's when I woke up.

I was startled, and I began to pray. "Lord, why did I have this dream? What are you trying to show me?"

I got out of bed and headed for the living room, where I sat down in my easy chair. When I did, it happened. I was outside of my body, suspended in space, far enough from the earth that I was able to look down at the earth. Then I saw them. Bright lights, angelic beings, hundreds of them. They were strategically placed all around the world. watchers! They were coming and going like flashes of light, going from their assigned place up to Heaven, then returning. Each one was assigned to keep an eye on what was going on in their specific area and then report that event to a higher-up there in Heaven. As I watched, it was all happening within a nano-second. Once the event was reported, the watchers would return to their assigned locations, while other angels were dispatched to that specific event.

As I was watching, many angels, perhaps hundreds, left Heaven and came to where the building had collapsed in my dream. As I watched, each angel went to a small child that had also died in the earthquake, picked them up in their arms, comforted them, and carried them away to Heaven. I was then swooshed away myself to Heaven, not inside of Heaven, but just outside of Heaven, to Paradise, where I watched as these children were delivered into the hands of other angels and those of the spirit bodies of some who had gone before. Their job was to love these children and train them in the ways of God, for they could not enter into Heaven until they were prepared. His presence would have been way too much for them to handle at this stage, just as those adults who came to accept His saving grace on their death beds couldn't handle Heaven until they were nurtured in the ways of God and in His presence. I assume this is also the case with babies that have been aborted. Having seen this, I now knew the purpose of the dream, and I was suddenly returned to my easy chair, not sure how long I'd been gone.

Journey Number 7

IN THE MOUNTAINS, CYBERIN, DAD, MERLE & BETTY

"Come on, let me show you some other things" the Lord said to me.

It was five a.m. on Sunday, November 5, 2017. I'd just finished a good night's sleep, so I was up and sitting in my easy chair. "Go ahead and call the traveling angel," He said.

When I did, my spirit body left my physical body, and out the front door I went. And like before, there was an angel waiting in the chariot for me. When he saw me, he just smiled, waited for me to get in the chariot, and off we went. As we were traveling, the thought occurred to me to ask him what his name was. He told me it was Cyberin. He told me there were all sorts of different angels with different assignments.

He said, "Some are created to be comforters, some warriors. Some have one set of wings, some three sets. Some are created to deliver messages, while others watch over the activities on earth. There are angels that worship, angels who sing, and those that visit, just to name a few. All of them are always busy doing something to serve the Master."

As we approached Heaven and I stepped out of the chariot, I was immediately met by three people. The first two were my dad and my father-in-law, both of whom I'd seen before. We had a wonderful time embracing, and I again asked them how they knew I was coming and where I would be landing.

They both looked at me and just smiled. "Here, you know so much more than when you were in the other life," my dad said.

The third person I saw was my mother-in-law. This was our first encounter since she'd passed, and I must admit she was just radiant. We embraced, and as I began to look closely at her, her face just glowed with the presence of the Lord. It was all over her. She appeared to be in her late twenties, possibly early thirties. She was very beautiful. For the first time, I looked down at someone's feet. She was wearing white, low-cut shoes with a very small heal, almost flat. We chatted about what she did there, and she told me she worked with children who came at an early age. As she placed her arm on mine, she told me that she spent time, as others did, teaching the children about the ways of God. She indicated that she really loved each and every one of them.

All three of them wanted to know where I was going this time, but since no one had come for me, I thought one of them might take me on a tour.

I looked over at the mountains and thought I'd like to see what it looked like there. I didn't remember saying goodbye to anyone, but all of a sudden I found myself up in one of the mountains I'd just looked at from afar. This was the first time I'd been transported somewhere simply by thinking about it. This place is just beautiful.

The first thing I noticed were the large green pine trees. There were other trees there, but the pines were the first I noticed. I looked around for fallen trees or dead trees. None were there. I couldn't find even one dead, fallen leaf. It was like a beautifully manicured park setting all around me for as far as I could see. Then I noticed a deer not too far from me, and an elk. Both were just grazing in the grass. They appeared to know I was there; however, neither one was alarmed by my presence. In the distance, I could see a black bear. My initial reaction was that the deer and elk should leave the area, because they are prime food for the bear.

As I was thinking that, the Lord spoke to me and reminded me that here the bears eat just like the deer and elk. Here, other animals had no fear of bears. In fact, He showed me that same bear down by the river. It was in the river playing with the fish, not eating them.

Then I was traveling by myself again. I flew back to the city, where I could see a very large building. To say the building was two hundred feet wide and two thousand feet long would be an understatement. As I landed, I found myself at the front door. Curious, I decided to go in. To my surprise, I saw rows and rows of body parts. Legs, hands, feet, all kinds of human body parts, just hanging there waiting for a purpose. I looked over to my left and saw two angels behind a counter. One was sitting while the other was standing. They appeared to be filling body-part orders from the miles and miles of spare body parts just waiting to be sent out from Heaven to people on the earth that needed them, but because of either their unbelief or the lack of prayer requests for these parts, no requests had come. Therefore, no orders to deliver them were being sent. I was so encouraged to see all of these in a readiness status, but saddened when I realized that very few knew they were there, as the two angels didn't look very busy.

Next, I traveled not too far, to a place near the throne. To the right of the throne, I could see the River of Life, which flowed from the throne to all over Heaven. Yet my attention was not directed to the right side of the throne as much, but to the left side. Below the throne flowed another river. It was not a river of water, yet it was a river. It was a river of new spirit bodies that had just been created for newborns on the earth. As I watched, they just kept flowing out of what might be called a fountain. As they came out, they went flying off to their recipients. It was a wonderful sight to watch.

I'm sure some would ask, "Well, how do you know that they went to newborns?" I can tell you that no one told me, but I just somehow knew.

At this point, my journey came to an end, and I found myself back in my easy chair. This time I had been gone for just under an hour.

Journey Number 8

THE THRONE ROOM &
ANGELIC COUNCIL

"Come on, let's go," the Lord said to me. It was Saturday afternoon, November 25, 2017. Donna, my wife, was out shopping, and the house was quiet. So off I went. I had not called for the traveling angel, so there was no chariot involved this time. I hadn't noticed this in previous departures, but this time as I was leaving earth and traveling out into space, I was surprised to see many satellites traveling around the earth. I was moving away from the earth, while at the same time, these satellites were traveling around the earth. I was surprised to see how many there were.

I didn't recall traveling any more, but I had now arrived. To my surprise, a welcoming committee was there. I still didn't know how they knew when I was coming or where I'd be arriving. They're explanation was that a person knows so much more there than in the former life. But now I saw them. My Dad greeted me with a heavenly hug. My brother Bill was also there, as were both of my in-laws, Merle and Betty, and my best friend Paul's wife, Paula.

We greeted each other, and my brother Bill said, "Sam, this place is awesome. It's so much better than hunting or fishing." (He'd been an outdoorsman with a passion for hunting and fishing in his former life.) Next was Paula. She said it was good to see me. I told her I had a message for her from Paul, her husband. He'd asked me to give it to her when I saw her. "He said to tell you he loves you, and he miss you a lot."

She said, "When you see him, tell him I love him, and I'll see him very soon."

I was reminded that those in Heaven have no concept of time, so soon could be tomorrow or many years from tomorrow.

As I was visiting with all of them, Jesus walked up to us, and we all begin to worship Him. When I saw Him, my knees buckled, and my face hit the floor. I was not sure what others were doing, because I was caught up in just worshipping Him while being in His presence.

He helped me to my feet and began to speak to me. "Sam, you're doing a good job. I have much to show you. You will be taking many more trips here, more frequently than you have so far. Things will begin to move faster now than they have before, but know that you are doing a good job. My servant Abraham will be coming soon to take you around again and show you things."

He acknowledged everyone again, and as He started to leave, I saw Abraham approaching. As we all greeted him, he told me we had much to see on this trip but that it wasn't time for me to see my home yet. We had other more pressing business to attend to. I said goodbye to everyone. They wished me well, and Abraham and I were off.

I don't recall how we traveled. I know it wasn't by chariot, but I did see that we were heading toward the great city. Perhaps it was by thought—Abrahams thought. I recall walking some inside of the city. Then we were in the center of the city, near the great throne. Outside, it appeared to be quiet. Abraham took me to the throne room. Peaking inside, I could see a part of it. It looked like a mighty boardroom for one of the greatest companies. I saw some of the elders' chairs. The ones I could see were all empty. I felt like I was on hallowed ground here, and there was a special presence I could actually feel. I'm not sure how long Abraham and I stood there, for in that presence, you just didn't want to move, much less leave. I was in awe of this place. Abraham told me it was time to leave. I felt like I must continually bow as we started to leave.

We walked a short distance, and he took me to yet another building. Inside was another boardroom. But it was filled with angels. I saw them coming and going. Some had wings; others didn't. Some seemed to be bringing messages, while others were receiving instructions.

"What is this place?" I asked.

"This is another heavenly council. This is where all the host of Heaven's angels come and go and report activities on the earth, in Heaven, and throughout the entire cosmos. From here, the council instructs all angels, and they receive assignments."

As I was watching, I saw what appear to be high-ranking military angels, who were given instructions regarding those under their command—yes, waring angels.

Angels were coming and going like this is a central command area. The council here received instructions from the throne room and implement these instructions through the comings and goings of this command center. There was so much activity here that I was mesmerized by all of it. So Abraham and I just stood there and watched for a long time. After that, it was time for me to return. My journey was over, and I once again found myself back in my easy chair, reflecting on what had just occurred and all that I had seen. I think I had been gone right about an hour. Amazing!

Journey Number 9

SINGING WITH THE
ANGELS & THE REDEEMED

I n the early afternoon of December 2, 2017, I called for the traveling angel, and before I knew it, there I was in the chariot with Cyberin, my traveling angel, at the helm. As we left the earth's atmosphere and began to travel out into space, I noticed the many satellites man had put into space as they were out there traveling around the earth.

Next, as before, I began to enjoy the view once again. As I did, I simply said, "Praise the Lord."

Cyberin repeated what I said. "Praise the Lord."

I said it again, and then he repeated it again. To my surprise, he began to sing a praise song to the Lord while I listened. He sang it in English so I could understand. Then, to my right, and outside of the chariot, another angel appeared. This angel began singing the song with Cyberin. Then on the left of the chariot, another angel appeared, and this one joined in with the praise song to the Lord. They continued the rest of the way into Heaven. As we were approaching, by this time I had learned a bit of the song, and I began praising the Lord with them in the song. But by the time we'd reached our destination, there were groups of angels both to my left and my right who were now singing the same song with us. Many citizens of Heaven also joined in, and we all became one large heavenly choir. It seemed like hundreds and hundreds were involved. No instruments were being played, and the harmony was simply "out of this world." I had not exited the chariot, but by now I was so involved with all of the others in praising the Lord that I'd risen to my feet and was singing in harmony with all the others, both angelic and redeemed. I couldn't stop, and when we would finish the song, if I started up again, everyone would just join in. I noticed some of the angels were singing in English, while others were singing in a heavenly language. Everyone harmonized, and it was glorious to say the least.

Before long, it was time for me to leave, and I found myself back in the living room. This short trip took only thirteen minutes. I love a good Gospel quartet as they harmonize with each other, or a wonderful rendition of a Christmas carol, but they don't compare in any way to the angelic choir.

Journey Number 10

Spirit of Christmas with the Angels

It's almost three o'clock in the afternoon on Friday, December 15, 2017. I heard the Lord say, "Come on, let's go."

I called for the traveling angel. "In the name of Jesus, I call the traveling angel to come and pick me up."

Instantly, while my physical body remained in the living room chair, my spirit body went out the front door and into the familiar chariot. Cyberin was there with a smile on his face, just like before. I sat down, he acknowledged me, and off we went. However, this time, as we traveled out from the earth's atmosphere and into outer space, he stopped the chariot, and we just stood still. I wondered why.

I began to look around and could not help but begin to see angels in large numbers coming from Heaven and traveling toward the earth. They were heading to places all over the earth. I asked Cyberin what was going on.

"Oh," he said. "These angels are busy getting ready to assist in the celebration of the birthday of our King. All over the earth, as well as in Heaven, we angels always get very excited as we prepare to celebrate King Jesus's birthday. He is King Jesus, our Master and the Lord of all. So, we never miss His birthday. Understand that on the earth, you humans always know when that day is, because you have designated a specific day as His birthday. However, in Heaven, we don't have a calendar. We feel that every day there with Him is a day of celebration. But we also know that on the earth, there is a special day appointed when you celebrate His birthday. You call it Christmas. So we come from Heaven in large numbers to join in the celebration with you. Angels are dispatched to places all over the earth for this."

I'd never thought of that. So here I was watching angels being dispatched from Heaven in large numbers, not going to the earth for the celebration but heading to earth for the preparation for the celebration. "What is it that they do?" I asked.

"When you return to earth, as you begin to look around, you will see them in action as you see the Spirit of Christmas in the faces of people. It's like light bulbs in a dark place being turned on to light up that place. You will see frowns being turned upside down as the joy of the Christmas Spirit catches them. That's what the angels are assigned to do all over the earth. Even wars stop for a period as they celebrate. Then, while there, we celebrate with you."

As I watched, they traveled at the speed of light, both going to the earth and returning to Heaven.

Next we traveled very fast through the galaxy to the center of everything—yes, Heaven. We didn't stop outside but went straight on in. As I began to step out of the chariot, I couldn't help but notice activities going on everywhere I looked. I wondered what they were doing. I noticed that both angels and the redeemed were heavily involved. This time, no one was there to greet me, so I inquired of my chariot driver, Cyberin, before he left.

"All of Heaven also celebrates King Jesus's birthday," he said. "Just like those who are still alive on earth do. Even though every day in Heaven is a joyous day, all of Heaven also celebrates the birthday of the King of Kings."

He informed me that angels had done this from the beginning, at His birth, and would continue to do so for all of eternity.

Everyone in Heaven looked so forward to it. I just stood there for a few moments and pondered just what everyone there could possibly be doing. After all, since nothing dies in Heaven, there were no dead leaves to rake up. There was no dust, so nothing appeared to need dusting. Since there was no wind, there was no trash that needed picked up, no garbage cans that needed emptying, and no windows that needed washing. Since nothing got tarnished, there was no need to polish anything. So what would all the commotion be from both the angelic realm and from those redeemed who were already there?

As I watched more closely, I realized no one was cleaning or polishing, or even straightening things up, for all things were as before, all in order as they should be. However, what everyone was doing, both angelic and the redeemed, was talking to each other and making sure everyone knew it was time for the King's celebration again. Those who already knew that the time was very near informed those who may have forgotten or had not yet known or experienced this wonderful celebration. There was excitement in the air. I was able to watch for a while, and then it was time for me to return to the earth and, once again, my physical body.

Journey Number 11

ABRAHAM & THE FUTURE
EVENTS BUILDING

I hadn't taken a trip for more than two weeks. However, on Thursday, January 4, 2018, at 2:20 in the afternoon, the Lord spoke to me and said, "Are you ready?"

"Yes," I said, and I called for the traveling angel. He arrived instantly. I climbed into the chariot, and off we went.

At first, I noticed that we didn't climb quickly through the earth's atmosphere but slowly drove through the clouds. It's one thing to fly through the clouds in an enclosed aircraft, but to travel through the clouds in an open chariot for a little while is a most invigorating experience.

We turned toward Heaven and quickly left earth's atmosphere and headed into outer space. We quickly picked up speed, for I noticed that the stars and planets became clusters of colors all mixed into the same scene. Then, before I knew it, we were there landing in Heaven.

I stepped out of the chariot and was soon greeted once again by Abraham. We embraced, and he told me it was good to see me again. Once again, his job was to show me around, and we departed not by chariot but on foot.

We came to a beautiful flower garden. It was very large, and it had flowers in colors I'd never seen before. The beauty and aroma from these flowers were out of this world. There are no words in the English language to describe them. Then Abraham pointed out a familiar face to me. It was Paul Robinett Sr. He looked like he was in his thirties—just great. As we said our hellos, he asked me about his son Paul. He wanted to know how he was doing. I said he was doing well and asked him if he knew that he'd gotten remarried. He looked at me as if he didn't understand. Abraham had to explain to me that, in Heaven, the concept of marriage, much less a second marriage is somewhat foreign, as everyone there treats everyone else with love, affection, and appreciation.

I explained to him that sometimes she had a bit of an elevated attitude and that she was working on that, along with some colorful language, but she was really good for him, and helped keep him in line.

We all laughed, and Ray said that it was good to see me. I kept wondering just what he was doing in a garden where nothing ever dies and weeds never grow, because in Heaven, the garden is always perfect. I remembered he always loved working in his garden back on the earth, so here he was, back doing what he always loved. It was just like the Father to see to even the smallest of details.

We left Ray and the garden and walked some distance to a building. I was not allowed to go in. Abraham told me the building was called the future events building. In it were held the end-time events spoken about in the last book of God's Word. These events were so troublesome that they were held in storage until their proper time. Even the angels were not allowed to go into the building until the time for the events to take place is right.

Finally, Abraham said he had a wonderful surprise for me. He then led me to my future home. It took my breath away. It looked like multiple domes, all combined. In the front was a circular driveway. At this time, since I was not allowed to go into it, I became curious about the circular driveway.

I asked Abraham, "Since we have no vehicles in Heaven, why the circular driveway?"

He explained that the Father knew all of my heart's desires and knew that I always wanted a home with a circular driveway. So He put one there just for asthetic purposes. I thought that was way cool.

Then it was time for me to leave. I thanked Abraham for the time we'd spent together. Then I headed home to my living room once again. It was now eight minutes after three. I'd been gone forty-eight minutes.

Journey Number 12

FACE-TO-FACE WITH JESUS

O n Tuesday, January 9, 2018, I took a wonderful trip. When I arrived in Heaven, I was standing outside the chariot for just a minute or two and was greeted by the King of Kings. When I saw him, I fell to the floor. He helped lift me up until I was face-to-face with him, and I was able to look into his eyes. I felt such warmth and peace. I can't find the words to describe the feeling of being there with Him.

We began to walk, not as though we were on a mission to go anywhere but walking as if we were taking a casual stroll. Jesus reached over to me and put his arm in mine. Imagine that. I was now walking arm-in-arm with the Creator of all things. It was a wonderful feeling, as though we had known each other for a long, long time and had been such good friends. He told me that I was doing a good job and that he had so much more yet for me to see and do.

I can tell you we strolled for what seemed like a lengthy time, and this time, unlike before, there were no interruptions. The balance of our conversation I'm not allowed to write about, except to say that it had to do with times and places, some too personal to mention, and that I'm honored that He shared these items with me. Then, it was time for me to return.

Journey Number 13

THE VISIT WITH MICHAEL
AND GABRIEL

On Thursday, January 18, 2018, and 11:10 in the morning, the house was quiet. I'd just finished studying for a new Bible study starting the following week. Now in my quiet time, I heard His voice. "Now would be a good time."

I agreed, and so I called for the traveling angel. Before I knew it, I was out the door. In the chariot, Cyberin had the biggest smile on his face that I'd ever seen. I was convinced he knew just what I was in for during this trip. As we sped off and traveled into outer space, I was just amazed at the beauty of the stars and planets—in fact, all of the cosmos. It was such a sight to behold. I wish everyone could see this magnificent wonder. It simply takes your breath away, with all of the vibrant colors that are there.

When we landed in Heaven and I stepped out of the chariot, I was surprised that no one was there to greet me. Therefore, I started walking by myself. At first, I didn't notice anything in particular. Then, as I was walking, people started walking up to me, or I would see them as they passed by and they would acknowledge me. "Good day," They'd say. "How are you doing?" Others would say, "It's good to see you again." Or, "Enjoying your stay?"

I couldn't help but wonder just how they knew who I was and why I was there. Then I thought maybe I was wearing something that signified to them that I was a stranger in this distant land. Or was my face all aglow? How did they know? Or did they just know?

I continued to walk for quite a while, all along still meeting smiling friendly faces. Just then, the angel Gabriel approached me. I'm not sure how I knew it was him, but I just knew. He was all of seven feet tall, and a very large angel. As he introduced himself, all of a sudden another very large angel approached. It was Michael. Both of them were standing right in front of me. At first, I couldn't get over their size. Both were wearing military armor, as if they were generals. Needless to say, I was extremely impressed. As we chatted, Gabriel reminded me of the host of angels that appeared in the sky on the eve of the birth of Christ, celebrating His arrival and singing, "Glory to God in the Highest." Gabriel told me he was there as part of the host.

Next, Michael reminded me of the time when the prophet Daniel had fasted and prayed for twenty-one days waiting on an answer (Daniel 10). Michael finally came and assisted the angel bringing the answer, as they together opposed the prince of Persia. When he said that, I was just blown away because I was thinking that the story in the book of Daniel happened well over twenty-five hundred years earlier. I was trying to get my head around the fact that I was standing face-to-face with the angel that was actually there at that time. Utterly amazing!

If that wasn't enough, both angels began to recall the all-Heaven party that took place just before Jesus left His position as King of Kings there in Heaven and came to the earth to be born as a human baby, knowing that He would ultimately sacrifice Himself for mankind. At the time, except for Enoch and Elijah (who never died, for God took them), all saints who had died didn't go to Heaven. They were sent to paradise, and they all knew what He was going to the earth to do. So they had this great sendoff party for Him before He left.

Standing there and looking at these two specimens of God's angelic creation, I could not get over how wonderful they looked. Not only magnificent in stature, but they were very beautiful to look at. In fact, I'd have to say they were absolutely gorgeous just to look at. Here before me stood not one but two of the three mightiest angels in charge of all of the angels of Heaven. And here they both were standing right in front of me. Wow! However, I didn't realize they were able to read my thoughts. They reminded me that they were just servants of the Most High like I was.

One of the things I noticed was that both Michael and Gabriel seemed to be studying me. I didn't have to ask them, for they indicated that only a handful of men had ever crossed over to this side and been allowed to return to the earth again, not just once, but several times. And so they were wondering what made me so different.

I assured them that I wasn't unique or different from most. I'd simply read the accounts of some who'd had the privilege of coming here and returning to the earth, and so one day while I was praying, I simply asked if others had gone, why couldn't I? The Lord's answer was simple: I'd simply never asked Him before. So, I asked if I could, and He said yes.

We spoke much of things taking place on the earth, especially those things that were related to both Israel and the church. They were interested to know specifics about the goings on on the earth; I was trying to glean from them what I could about this place called Heaven. We spoke for quite a while, and then it was time for me to leave again. When I returned, it was a few minutes after twelve p.m. I'd been gone just under one hour.

Journey Number 14

ALL THE WAY IN TIME
WITH JESUS

O n Saturday, January 27, 2018, at 2:10 in the afternoon, I took one of the most unusual trips ever. The journey started the same as most of the other journeys—with the chariot and driver picking me up out in the front yard. However, when I arrived in Heaven, we landed fairly near the throne area. To my surprise, there was no one there to meet me or instruct me as to what we were going to see or do.

I didn't move very far from where we'd landed, and standing outside of the throne area. While I looked around at all of the surroundings, I was met by the King of Kings Himself. When I saw Him, I fell to the floor. After a short while, He helped me to my feet. I'll never forget His eyes—so deep with love and compassion. Being in His presence was everything. I could stop there and say I didn't need to see or do anything else, but then He put His right arm around my shoulder and said that during this trip, I would be taken on a journey of time and space.

The Father wanted me to go backward from today, first, to the New Testament era. After I'd looked around, recalling moments of that time, we went to our second destination—the period when the Old Testament was. Then, we went back further in time to our third destination: the time when Moses lived. Fourth, we visited the time of Abraham. Our fifth visit was to observe events during Adam and Eve's time. After He showed me all of these times, I thought we were done. Wow, was I ever surprised. The sixth visit to see all of those things that made up the beginning of creation on the earth. From there, He took me to the seventh destination, to see the creation of those items that were created outside of the earth, that being other planets in our solar system, to include creation of the sun and the moon. He reminded me that before the sun and moon were created, time was not a factor. So when He created the sun and moon, He also implemented the concept of time.

Our eighth destination was outer space—other galaxies, planets, and stars and the creation of each. Our ninth excursion took me to Heaven, and I learned when and how He created it. Finally, the tenth destination was to see His creation of His angelic army.

By this time, my head was spinning, and I was sure that He was done. I thought there was nothing left to show me that existed or that had been created. But I was wrong. At last, He took me to that period before any of His creations, when all that was there was God in the stillness of the dark. That is the way it was before time or anything else existed. Only God was there, and God alone. He always was and always will be.

It was now my time to return to my easy chair in the living room. I must confess that I was having difficulty trying to get my head around all of what I have just witnessed and experienced.

Journey Number 15

APOSTLE PAUL AND
MEETING RACHEL

On Thursday, February 8, 2018, just after three p.m., I returned from a most unusual trip, which lasted just under an hour. I was sitting in my easy chair when I heard His voice. It was very easy to recognize.

He said, "Come on, let's go," and away we went.

No chariot or traveling angel this time, I just left and was almost instantly there. When I arrived in Heaven, I didn't recognize the place, as I hadn't been in this particular part of it before. However, I soon saw the apostle Paul sitting on a bench. How I knew it was him, I didn't know, but I just knew. He was reading the Word. As I approached him, my earthly Father also soon approached. We greeted one another, and then I met Paul. He seemed to be quite an intelligent man, not very big in stature, and Dad and he also greeted each other. I was told they'd had many sessions together discussing the elements of the Word.

Paul was curious to know just how I was getting along and if I needed anything or whether there was anything that he could do for me while I was there. I thanked him and assured both he and my father that I was being well looked after. Then both men were interested in how the church was doing back on the earth. I told them that the Gospel was being spread all over the earth and that many souls were coming to Christ every day. That statement put smiles on both of their faces.

I felt as though the Lord was pulling me away from the two of them, so I said my goodbyes to both and slowly started to walk away.

Then the Lord spoke to me. He was not standing next to me, yet somehow I could hear His voice. "I have a surprise for you," He said. Then I heard another voice from behind me. When I heard this voice, somehow I instantly knew who it was. She simply said one word: "Daddy"

As I turned to see who it was, she spoke to me again. "HI, Daddy." She put her arms around my neck to give me the biggest hug and kiss. She was my daughter. It was now forty years ago, that my wife, Donna, had been pregnant. However, in her third month, she had a miscarriage, and we lost the baby. Yet, here I was standing in front of this beautiful woman who appeared to be in her early thirties, calling me daddy, and I instantly knew she was my daughter, the child we'd lost all those years ago. She had dark brown hair like her grandmother and hazel eyes, just like her mother. Her stature was not as small as her mother's but not quite as large as mine. She was very beautiful and had an infectious smile.

We sat down on a bench and just held each other's hands. She told me she had anxiously waited until this day to meet me. Not too long ago, she had met and gotten to know her grandparents on her mother's side, and indicated that she'd spent quite a bit of time with my dad. She said he got the biggest smile on his face and just beamed when she called him Grandpa. One of his jobs was to help teach her in the ways of God, so they had spent much time together once he'd gotten there. Up until that time, she had been taught by some of those who had come there earlier as well as some of the angels.

"I'm so proud of you for the work that you are doing," she said. "A lot of people here, including some of the angels, know what you're doing."

I was surprised to hear her say that.

"Please tell my mother that I said hello and that I love her and look forward to seeing her soon," she said. "Also, how is my brother doing?"

I told her he was doing fine, that he loved the Lord, and that he had a passion for the study of God's Word.

"Please tell him that I said hello," she said. "And that I can't wait to meet him and spend some time together, just the two of us."

Even though I didn't want to, I felt that it was almost time for me to go. "What do they call you here?" I said. "Do you have a name?"

"No," she said. "You never named me before I left, so I've been without an earthly name."

"I think I would like to call you Rachel, if that's all right with you. I'll have to check with your mother to see if it's okay with her as well."

She said that was okay, and then a large smile came on her face as she realized she had an earthly name. We hugged once again, kissed, and said our goodbyes.

Before, I thought I was torn between two worlds, wanting to stay here, yet knowing I needed to go back, but now I was really torn, for I really didn't want to leave this place. I must confess that being able to see loved ones in both places was extremely hard. I felt like I need to be cloned.

Journey Number 16

TO PERSONAL TO WRITE

This trip was so personal that I cannot write about it.

Journey Number 17

OUT OF THIS WORLD

This trip was so "out of this world" that I simply do not have the words to describe it. When God gives me the right words, I'll tell of this journey.

Journey Number 18

JESUS AND THE CITY OF DEATH

On Tuesday, March 27, 2018, at 2:17 p.m., I arrived home from a journey to Heaven that lasted approximately one and a half hours.

I'd been sitting in my living room when I heard Him calling me, and so out the front door I went to my awaiting chariot. The ride to Heaven was uneventful, except that, as in the past, the sights were just amazing.

I landed in Heaven, and shortly after I stepped out of the chariot, I was met by the Master himself. When I recognized who He was, once again I fell to the floor in worship. As before, He assisted me to my feet, and motioned me to a bench nearby, where we (just the two of us) could sit and talk.

I wanted to know what His last week or so on the earth was like, from His perspective. He started with His triumphal ride into Jerusalem on a young donkey.

"Even though I knew all that was to come over the course of the next few days, I was just so full of joy as I rode the donkey into the city square. People were singing, 'Hosanna, blessed is He who comes in the name of the Lord.' They were ready to crown me their King, waving palm branches and cheering. It was a great time of celebration, at least until we arrived at my Father's House, the temple. However, once I saw the money changers and all the business that was being conducted in the name of My

49

Father, I was infuriated, especially as some were taking advantage of others less able. My anger raged as I drove them all out of the temple square. I was embarrassed for My Father and could not let it stand.

"I was so moved with compassion as I saw countless people who were sick, lame, and blind while I was spreading my Father's Word. I just loved seeing them set free from those ailments. I especially liked seeing those who were possessed by demons as they were set free.

"I knew my arrest was soon coming, and I relished the time I had left with my disciples. Sitting with them at the last supper and then serving them while washing their feet was a special blessing to me, and I was sure some received the servanthood message.

"The arrest in the garden was very troubling for Me, as I knew that those who had been with me for the last three years would now be scattered. It was for them that I had prayed, as well as for those who were doing their duty while not really knowing what they were doing.

"Standing before Pilot, well, he knew I was not the normal trouble-maker he was used to seeing. It was interesting to see him try and figure out just who I was. However, when I was taken away by the guards and ridiculed, whipped, beaten, and tortured, remember that I was as much in my natural body as you are when you're back on the earth. After the guards whipped me, they ripped parts of my beard out by hand and placed a thorny crown upon my head. I never felt so much pain, but I remained faithful to my mission. I knew when I stood before the crowd that they were fulfilling the Father's plan for me as they yelled, 'Crucify him.' I was pretty weak and numb as I made My way out of the city while carrying the cross. By then it was too much, and I fell. One of the guards made one of the bystanders carry it the rest of the way to the top of the hill.

"By the time that they laid me onto the cross my body was already pretty numb; however, driving the spikes through my body was an indescribable experience. The pain was everywhere.

"There I was on the cross, knowing that I was paying the price for the sins of all mankind, and yet, there the adversary was standing by me just mocking me, and laughing. He was convinced that he had finally won, and when I said "it is finished," he and a band of his could do nothing but rejoice.

"In that moment there on the cross, My spirit body left My physical body, and I watched as they took me down from the cross. It was then that my adversary began to realize that this was not the end, but the beginning.

"As they laid my body in the tomb, I had not yet ascended to my Father. Yet, I could hear all of Heaven cheering, as they knew what I was about to do.

"Down I went to the city of death, in Hades, or Sheol, to the temporary place of the dead. I stood for just a moment in front of the gates of the city. They were closed, so I tore them off of their foundations and entered. Off to my left was Paradise, or Abraham's Bosom, the place of temporary rest for the righteous. As my presence became known, a great time of shouting and cheering began. I informed them that I'd come to take them with me out of that place to a better place. However, there was one more place I had to go first. I left Paradise and went back to Hades proper. There I visited the spirits in prison and preached to those of Noah's time. Then I led those from Hades proper, who accepted my message, along with all of Paradise out of Hades/ Sheol and took them all along with me to my Father's home in Heaven, where they were presented to the Father.

"I had not been presented to my Father yet, because I still had much to do on the earth. It was now early in the morning of the third day. My Father assigned two angels to the tomb where my physical body had been lying. As My spirit body reentered my physical body, my Father breathed life back into my physical body, and as I took my first breath. The angels rolled the stone away from the tomb. I put garments on, and walked out for the first time.

"Meeting the two Mary's on the way back to the city was a delight, especially once they realized who I was and that I had fulfilled my resurrection promise. I could see that they were filled with much joy and excitement as they ran back to tell others that they had seen Me once again and that I was alive, just as I had said I would be.

"I enjoyed gathering in the upper room with most of those who had been with me through the last few years, plus now there were also new believers. I just appeared to them, and they were overwhelmed and full of excitement as they looked at my hands, feet, and side and realized I'd been resurrected, just as I'd said I would be. Then I equipped them as I breathed on them to receive the Holy Spirit.

"It was time for me to present myself to My Father. So off I went, and there, in front of the host of angels, along with those from Paradise and the newly redeemed, I presented myself to Him. As I put on my Royal Robe and Crown and stood to the right of the Father, the Heavenly cheer there was all inspiring, for all of Heaven knew what had been accomplished.

"A few days later, I appeared to the disciples once again, in a closed room. Thomas was there, so I encouraged him to touch my hands and my side so he would believe and not doubt. Overall, I appeared to the disciples on three separate occasions, and during the forty days I was there, I was seen by over five hundred followers. Then, once again, it was time for me to leave and take my rightful place in Heaven next to my Father."

When He had finished telling me of His experiences of His last week and more while on the earth, I told Him I had a much clearer understanding of all that had taken place during those last days. I thanked the Lord for the time we'd spent together. He told me He'd picked the right person for this job.

Then it was time for me to leave, and my chariot arrived. As I climbed into the chariot, I turned around to say goodbye to Him, but He was already talking with someone else. I didn't know who it was. After I climbed in, away we went, and before too long, I found myself once again in my easy chair in the living room. As I said earlier, I had been gone about one and a half hours.

Journey Number 19

GREAT OUTDOOR GATHERING
AT THE THRONE AREA

I went on a trip for a short while on Tuesday, April 24, 2018, beginning at 10:44 a.m. I was sitting in my easy chair, and I called for
the traveling angel to come and pick me up. In one quick moment, my
spirit body left my physical body, and out the front door I went. There
it was, just as before, the chariot and driver waiting for me. Cyberin
acknowledged me with a nod and a beautiful smile. Soon I was nestled
in the chariot, and we were off.

As we sped off, I looked at the clouds with some interest in their
beauty this time. They looked just like soft white pillows, and I enjoyed
looking at them at first from below, then while we were in them, and
finally, as we were speeding away from them. I remarked to myself
that they looked different from each point of view—beautiful, but
different.

Next, as we moved through outer space, I could see certain planets.
I wasn't sure which ones they were, but it caused me to turn and see
Earth at a distance. I think, of all the planets, without a doubt, the earth
is the most beautiful and picturesque, with its different whites, greens,
blues, etc.

Moving along at increasing speeds, I was and still am mesmerized by the galaxy, with its layout, shapes, clusters of stars, and vibrant
colors. The beauty of it is just breathtaking. When you look at this, it's

simple to see that this did not just happen on its own but was wonderfully created by a Mastermind who knew exactly where to put each piece of the puzzle.

Upon arriving in Heaven, we didn't stop where we had previously stopped. Cyberin must have been instructed to take me very close to the great outdoor gathering area close to the throne, for when we landed, I immediately heard a huge crowd cheering from the throne area. I wasn't very far from there, so I just walked toward the noise.

As I approached, I could see an enormous crowd of people and angels mixed together. They were all standing around the throne area. I could see Jesus standing in the middle of what looked like a stage. Obviously, He was preaching and teaching. As I listened, I realized His message was not about ongoing things there in Heaven, but about issues that either were currently ongoing on the earth, or future events that were to take place on the earth. He didn't seem concerned with the issues. He was more interested in the people the Father had given him but were not presently with Him—Those still living on the earth who would have to be dealing with those things currently happening or yet to come, and He was instructing all those before Him to earnestly pray for those that eventually would become brothers and sisters. His message was quite intense, and everyone listening realized this was their task for the present time. As He spoke, He shared how much He loved each one there, and He included those yet to join Him there. Therefore, His message was straight forward. When I listened, I knew exactly what He was speaking about and the assignment at hand. In addition, I understood, as I was sure all those present did, that this assignment was to be carried out until all those who were yet to come home had. His message was simple, direct, and to the point.

Then it was time for me to return to Earth and my easy chair, which held my physical body. I'd only been gone for about fifteen minutes.

Journey Number 20

FAMILY ENCOUNTER & GRANDMA V.

O n Wednesday, May 16, 2018, my trip started at 1:55 p.m. Once again, I was in my easy chair in the living room. I called for the traveling angel. While my spirit body got up, my physical body stayed behind in the chair, and out the front door I went to my awaiting chariot and driver, Cyberin. Once again, he nodded a hello to me, and he had a huge grin on his face. As we sped off into space, even though the trip this time didn't take long, I must admit, as on some previous trips, I was just mesmerized by the beauty of all of the stars, planets, and the Milky Way. To say all of this was so breathtaking, well, it just doesn't do justice to its magnitude, beauty, or splendor.

As I landed in Heaven, I remarked to myself that I'd been to this spot before. After I'd exited the chariot, my driver once again acknowledged me with a nod of his head, and off he went.

Standing there with no one else around, I began to hear the Master speak to me—not vocally this time, but telepathically. He reminded me of many but not all of the places I'd visited on previous journeys. Some of which were the mountains; forests; rivers; streams; lakes; fields of wild flowers, Paradise, the great wall that surrounded all of Heaven, with its foundations and colors; the New City Jerusalem, all prepared and just there in waiting; the throne room, where the twenty-four elders sit; the meeting place where Jesus spoke to the masses; the spare human parts building; the angel assignment room; and my new mansion, which I'd been allowed to go and stand in front of but not enter. As He spoke to me about each one, I was instantly taken back to them individually, and for a brief moment, I was able to bask in the joy I'd felt as I visited each and every one of the places. All I could do was thank and praise Him for allowing me to take these journeys and experience each and every one of the places I'd been to.

As I was standing there, Merle, my father-in-law, approached me. We greeted with a hug.

"It is so good to see you again," He said.

I was interested in what occupied Him a good portion of the time there. I asked him if he had a job there and, if so, what it was. He said he was the keeper of some of the gardens. That surprised me because I knew there were no weeds anywhere in Heaven, nor was there any type of death. Therefore, he would not be required to weed the flowers or pull dead or dying plants, so what was he talking about? Then he told me that one of his jobs was to pick flowers and place them in certain places around the city. After he'd pulled a flower out of the ground, a new flower instantly grew to replace it, so that the gardens always remained in perfect order. As he was telling me about his duties, he had the biggest smile on his face, and he told me he just loved doing what he did.

While we were standing there, my dad approached. We said hello and hugged. He wanted to know how I was getting along with the work I was called to do. He already knew the answer from Heaven's point of view, but he wanted to know the answer from mine. I assured him that all was right on schedule. Then I asked him what he'd been doing since we'd previously seen each other. He said he continually attended a study of God's ways with several other men there, and that it was taught by the apostle Paul. He said it was often a "spirited study." In addition, he had the honor of teaching Bill, his son, and one of my brothers, in the ways of God. Usually very young believers are taught these ways in Paradise by others trained to do so. Instead, he had the privilege of doing so with Bill. I was so excited to hear that and wanted to see Bill and speak with him, but he did not attend this trip.

Next, my mother-in-law, Betty, approached. She was such a beautiful woman, but had I not been in my spirit body, I wouldn't have recognized her. However, my spirit body instantly recognized her, and we embraced. She told me it was good to see me again, and I told both her and my father-in-law that I had a message for both of them from one of their daughters, Susie. She had asked me to give them a message from her when I saw them next. She said to tell them hi from her and that she loved them both very much. They both seemed to soak that in like a sponge. Then they both said to tell both girls they loved them very much and looked forward to seeing them soon. I then asked her if she was still training the young children in the beginning ways of God, and she nodded yes. And she told me she just loved what she was doing.

As I was standing there with these people, my daughter Rachel approached. Wow, what a pretty woman she was, with her dark hair and hazel eyes—just like her mother. She put her arms around my neck and said, "Hi, Daddy, it's so good to see you again." Next, she gave Merle a hug around his neck and said, "Hi, Grandpa." He smiled from ear to ear.

Next, she approached my farther. She put her arms around his neck and hugged him. "Hi, Grandpa," she said. I couldn't contain myself. I looked at both of my fathers. They were both beaming.

I mentioned to Rachel a number of places I'd seen, and I indicated to her that I had been taken to see my Heavenly home but up to now hadn't been allowed to enter it.

"Oh," she said. "You're not allowed in there until a certain time. Did you know that the glory of God fills that place? So, it's not empty." If you were allowed to enter it, you couldn't stand in it."

Then she introduced herself to Betty, my mother-in-law. From that, I understood that they had not met before, or if they had, it had been some time since they have seen each other.

Then to my surprise, up walked another beautiful woman that, in the natural, I would not have recognized. However, in the spirit, I did. It was my grandmother Rose, my mother's mother. As we embraced, she kissed me and said, "Hello, Sammy." She was the only one who ever called me by that name. She had very long black hair that ran halfway down her back. She was about five foot three. Of all of my grandparents, I liked her the most, and I think she did me too. So we just hung on and hung on to each other. It was so good to see her.

Cyberin came with the chariot then, and I knew it was time for me to leave. After saying goodbye to everyone, I climbed into the chariot, and, waving to each and all of them, we were off. But to my surprise, we didn't leave Heaven. Instead, Cyberin took me to my mansion. I got out of the chariot and was able to walk up to it. I tried to look inside one of the windows, but the interior was filled with either a cloud or smoke. Therefore, I couldn't see anything inside. Next, I went around to the other side and tried to peek inside, but just like before, I was unable. I just went to the front, and for a few brief moments I just stood out front to take in the view. It was an amazing looking structure.

Then I climbed back into the chariot, and away we went. It didn't seem to take very long to return to Earth and to my physical body in the easy chair. However, once again, the view leaving Heaven and passing through the galaxy was just breathtaking. Along with all of its colors, I saw Earth first as a small dot, which quickly grew larger and larger. That was really enjoyable. About then it was over, and I was once again back in my physical body, sitting in the easy chair. I looked at the clock. It was 2:35. I'd been away about forty minutes.

DAD AND THE HEAVENLY
ANGELIC CHOIR

O
n Thursday, June 21, 2018, I returned from a forty-five minute trip, which started at 12:35 p.m. I had called for the traveling angel to come in Jesus's name. As my spirit body left my physical body, out the front door I went to the chariot and driver. After I'd taken my seat in the chariot, he turned to see that I was ready to go, he acknowledged me with his infectious smile, and off we then went. Unlike trips that I'd taken with him before, this time I was more than curious as to how he was driving the chariot, so I leaned forward to look in front of him. I didn't see a steering wheel, steering laterals, or push buttons. So how was he able to direct the chariot to where he wanted to go? I asked him. To my surprise, he didn't speak. He only pointed to his head.

"Do you mean you're directing the chariot telepathically?" I said.

With a smile, he nodded. All I could do was sit back and enjoy the ride and its unbelievable view, while thinking about some of the possibilities utilizing that kind of ability.

As before, the trip didn't take very long, and upon arriving in Heaven, I saw my dad waiting for me. As I exited the chariot, I waved goodbye to Cyberin. As Dad and I hugged, he said, "It's good to see you again." He directed me toward a certain portion of the great city. I wanted to sit down with him and hear about what he'd been doing since we spoke last and from the beginning of his arrival here. However, rather than sit and talk, we continued to walk while we talked. It became obvious to me that he was excited to get us to a certain place. He told me about how much he'd loved teaching my brother Bill in the ways of God, while still attending further studies of God's Word with the apostle Paul, as well as a few other men. He said it had become much easier to understand certain studies that had confused him while he was still on the earth. I surmised that many who are there had a much greater and easier understanding of the Word than they had before, and I said I was looking forward to that.

We were still quite a distance away from the place where he was taking us, I began to realize where he was taking me as I started to hear music. The closer we got to where we were heading, the louder the music became. Then, all of a sudden, there they were. I was now standing in front of the Heavenly angelic choir. Yes, I mean a huge amount of them. It looked like literally hundreds and hundreds of angels. Could have been thousands; I couldn't tell. There they were all gathered together, singing what I assumed were praises unto the Father, His Son, and His precious Spirit. However, I didn't understand the words, as they were singing in a Heavenly language. I was able to make out a few words from my own prayer language, but I just knew they were worshipping the Trinity. It was awesome, to say the least. Dad knew many of the songs, so he sang and worshipped along with others. Worship in Heaven is very, very different than it is here on the earth.

While I was standing there with my dad, I could hear musical instruments being played, but I was never able to see an orchestra anywhere. The music and the choir just engulfed me, as I guess it also did my dad, so we just stood there worshipping together while this massive heavenly choir sang.

I wasn't sure just how long we stood there, because time didn't seem to be a factor. We were just engulfed in the presence of it all, and I can say that I didn't want to leave. The glory of God just filled the air. There were times when I was so overwhelmed, I was unable to speak.

The choir was still singing, but eventually it was time for me to leave. I didn't know how I knew it was time. Maybe dad knew. As we walked off, I felt as though I was floating in a cloud of the Father's glory. Finally, we approached Cyberin and the chariot. As Dad and I said our goodbyes, I didn't feel as though I needed a chariot or a driver. I felt I could have journeyed myself. Now, I was off again, heading back to Earth, soon to be returning to my physical body, which awaited me in the easy chair in the living room. It was now 1:20 p.m.

Journey's Number 22 and 23

THE GALAXIES AND
WARING ANGELS

D ue to the nature of the last two trips, I have chosen to incorporate both of these trips into just one section. In the first of the two trips, number 22, I was picked up in the chariot by Cyberin. We left the earth, but I never made it to Heaven, as the entire trip was spent out into space among the stars, planets, cosmos, galaxies, etc.

Traveling around other planets and what seemed like millions and millions of stars that were clustered together into an unbelievable array of colors that were all blended together, well I have a difficult time trying to describe its beauty. I don't think the English language has adequate words to describe it, for it is literally out of this world.

Next, we traveled far into outer space, where I could see many other galaxies, literally hundreds and hundreds of them (maybe millions). It was not only awesome to see, but I'm still trying to get my head around this fact. Literally, I think it will take all of eternity to discover all of these galaxies. I was convinced we'd have to be in our glorified bodies to experience this, as each one would require a lifetime to explore and appreciate.

During trip number 23, I was not picked up in the chariot. It was early in the morning. I was lying in bed visiting with the Lord and heard His voice say, "Come up here."

Instantly, I was there in Heaven. No one was waiting for me, and I didn't go to see anyone I knew. However, the Lord wanted to educate me regarding a portion of His angels. Specifically, He wanted to teach me about His waring angels. They are a specific group of angels. All of them were quite large and extremely well-built. They looked like they were built for battle. As I looked at them more intently, I didn't see a glow about them as I'd seen on other angels; however, they did have an aurora about them, in different colors. Some were brighter than others. The Lord explained to me that the different colors represented different degrees of office. Just as in most militaries, there were privates, corporals, captains, generals, etc. In the waring angel army, there were soldiers that had different degrees of office, and they were identified by the different colors of the aurora on each one. As an example, a waring angel with a gold aurora is a general. I was curious as to why He would be teaching me this about His waring angel army. He told me it was specifically for end-time knowledge. He said during these end times, we'd encounter angels and would be able to know who they were and their positions, offices, etc. Then I was sent back home.

Journey Number 24

CABIN IN THE MOUNTAINS

At about 2:25 p.m. on Saturday, July 28, 2018, my spirit body left my physical body and the easy chair in the living room. I journeyed very quickly through outer space to the mountains in Heaven. During this trip, I didn't travel with the help of Cyberin or chariot. Instead, I simply heard His voice, and I found myself instantly there. It seemed to happen in a twinkling of an eye.

The mountains looked much like those on the earth, except that there was nothing dead there. Therefore, I didn't see a fallen tree, dead bushes, or brown leaves. In fact, the place looked like it was just manicured and was just gleaming with its own ability to worship the Master.

I was not standing at the bottom of the mountains, for I could see down from where I was standing. However, I was standing at the edge of a large lake in the mountains in a substantial green forest of large pines, oaks, and other trees and next to a large body of water. It was an indescribable breathtaking sight. I realize the English language just doesn't do it justice. This beauty was just a small bit of the Creators handiwork.

Off to my right and slightly down the shore, there stood a beautiful, modern looking log cabin. As I was standing there enjoying its setting and beauty, I heard His voice again. "I have created this for you to enjoy whenever you want. It is your second home here. I know how much you enjoy the mountains, so I created this just for you."

I was overwhelmed, to say the least. I didn't recall Him telling me to go inside, but I remember standing inside looking out at the lake. Wow, what a view. The ceiling was high and vaulted and was all made of wood. It was beautiful, and the wall facing the lake was made of glass, except for the framework, so that the view would never be hidden. The inside was furnished in just my taste.

I asked Him, "Will Donna come here?" His answer was yes. I went outside to the large front porch so I could just take in the beauty of the lake view. The wraparound porch was quite large. There were steps on each side, and the main set of steps cascaded down part of the way to another set of smaller porches at ground level. It was very impressive.

Then He said, "There are many here that have second homes in these mountains. They love being here just as much as you do. And remember, if you want to, you can walk out on the water, just like I did. If you want to, you also have the ability to walk under the water."

I was overwhelmed. I didn't look into a kitchen area, but I did look into what I would call the formal dining area. I mentioned to myself that it also had glass to the one side of it, so as you would sit at the table you'd also be able to look out onto the lake view.

I wasn't sure just how long I was there. Then it was time for me to return to Earth and my physical body, waiting for me in the easy chair of the living room. I was gone about twenty-five minutes.

I didn't want to leave, and I so desire to go back again. Heaven is so very real!

Journey Number 25

JESUS, MY ADVOCATE
WITH THE FATHER

O n Friday, August 17, 2018, at about ten in the morning, I was sitting in my easy chair. I thought, "This would be a good time to take a trip." So I called for Cyberin to come and pick me up in Jesus's name. In an instant, my spirit body moved from the chair and out the front door. In the front yard was Cyberin. He was just sitting in the hovering chariot. He looked at me and smiled as I climbed in. Then, without saying a word, we were off. I just sat back and enjoyed the trip once again. As we traveled through space, the galaxy was, as usual, just glistening with breathtaking beauty. All I could do was marvel at this handiwork of God.

When I arrived in Heaven, I saw that a considerable group of saints was just waiting for me to arrive. Again, I was somewhat awestruck. I wondered how they knew I was coming. Out of all of Heaven, how did they know just where I would be landing. Somehow, they just knew.

Many of the people there had been in Heaven for quite some time, so I didn't know them. Yet they were curious, I guess, to see me and see just who this person was that was permitted to cross over for a short period of time and then be allowed to cross back. Some of them wanted to hear about things going on the earth ever since their departure. I on the other hand wanted to find out from them about things going on in Heaven. Needless to say, I did not win this battle, as we discussed many topics since World War II, including the outcome of that war, as some had died fighting in it. What could I tell them about events on the earth during the last seventy-plus years? Some wanted to know if I knew any of their relatives—parents, grandparents, siblings—and if I would be allowed to take a message back with me to some of them from those here. I told them I wasn't sure, as prior to this meeting, I hadn't been asked by strangers. However, the most common theme I heard was that they all wanted me to tell those still alive on the earth that Heaven is a very real place, and that these relatives and friends who were standing before me were very much alive. To those standing before me, that seemed to be the most important issue.

As I was talking with this group (maybe thirty or so), Abraham came by. Many in the group acknowledged him with a hello, and he told me he'd come to take me to a very important meeting. So we said our goodbyes to the group, thanking them for coming, and Abraham and I walked away. We talked for a little bit while we walked and he informed me that I had an appointment with the Father and His Son (Jesus). We continued for a time and soon came to the throne room. I was not permitted to go inside, and once we arrived, I never looked up. As I was standing there, Jesus came up and stood beside me to my left. He told me He was my advocate with the Father and would speak for me to the Father. First of all, I was not clear on what I should say, if anything, or what I should do, but I was very blown away by the fact that Jesus was standing beside me. Just realizing that made my knees buckle, and to also realize that He was my personal advocate with the Father. Wow, He was going to represent me. First, standing in front of the throne, I didn't think I could have spoken, even if I was asked, but then I realized that here standing with me was Jesus, my personal advocate who would be representing me. It gave me such a feeling of confidence. I was not able then, and still have not been able, to get my head around this fact, to think about and realize that Jesus is with me everywhere, including this home here in Heaven.

As we were standing there, He spoke with the Father. "Father, here stands Samuel. I have brought him before you at your request. He has been washed clean through my blood and continues to work on the project assigned to him by You. I have brought him before You because I know there are some things You want to say to him."

Without looking up, I could hear a crackling like lightning bolts in the background. While still looking down, I could see the reflections of colors — gold, red, emerald green, blue, and purple. What I thought of was that it must be a rainbow that was surrounding the Father. I expected to hear a deep, strong voice, but to my amazement what I heard was a still small gentle voice. However, it was not an audible one, but an inner one that was coming from within me and conversing with my own spirit.

"Have you been enjoying these short trips while working on the project for Me, and have you been happy with what you have been seeing and learning while here?" He asked. "Have you enjoyed seeing My handiwork while you have traveled through space and time? You have met patriarchs that you have read about, seen relatives and friends that have been here with Me for a while and heard their particular stories. I have invited some of them to show you various places here, and you have even listened to my angelic choir as they have entered into times of worshipping me, and in some of those times, I have watched as you have entered into worship with them. All of that has been very pleasing to Me. You have been doing a good job, but there is so much more that I want you to see and learn about here, so that you are able to share that which you have learned about with those of my children who are still alive and on the earth today. All power and authority is given unto my Son, and soon He will harvest the earth to join those here, for the great feast of the redeemed.

"Do not worry about what to do with all of what you have seen and learned, for at the right time, I will put the proper people into your path, for I have also appointed them for this time. They will know what to do. As a result of what you are doing, know that I have placed a hedge around you."

When the Father was done, Jesus thanked Him, and we left His presence. Then it was time for me to return to the earth and my physical body. I don't recall the trip back, because I was engulfed in what I had just experienced. I once again found myself back in my body sitting in the easy chair. The clock said it was 10:39 a.m. I had been gone over a half an hour.

One of the questions that has come up is about time. Is it the same in Heaven as it is in the earth? In other words, is five minutes on the earth the same as five minutes in Heaven? My answer: I don't know, but since time in Heaven is not a factor (no sunrise and no sunset), it could be that much more is accomplished in Heaven during the same amount of time. This is just my observation.

Journey Number 26

THE GREAT WALL
SURROUNDING HEAVEN

At about two forty-five on Thursday, August 23, 2018, I returned from a twenty-minute trip.

In all of the trips I've taken, I have continually been curious about the great wall that surrounds all of Heaven and its purpose. During my one-on-one time with the Lord, I asked Him, "Why is there a huge wall surrounding all of Heaven? After all, since believers are free to arrive here, and no unbelievers can ever enter, those angels who didn't leave in the Great Fall could be the only other creatures that could possibly enter. Therefore, why is there this huge wall that surrounds all of Heaven?" I guess it was time for my lesson.

His said, "There are three types of the Father's creation that have been allowed to enter into Heaven. First are those who are the redeemed righteous. They consist of mankind, all the way back to the time of Adam and down through time and even until I return to the earth the next time. These are the ones that I bought and paid for when I shed my blood on Calvary. In addition, they will include any new believers who accept and receive Me as their personal savior during My one thousand year reign on the earth. This will occur just prior to God's great white throne judgment. To these, the great wall that surrounds all of Heaven does not have a purpose.

"Next who exist are all of the Father's angelic creations who are still serving Him, which are the remaining two-thirds of the angels who didn't choose to follow Satan at the beginning of time and during the Fall. They come and go as they have always been assigned. To them, the wall has no specific meaning or purpose.

"Finally is the one-third of all the angels that chose to follow and worship Satan. They are divided into two groups. The first group includes those angels who took woman for themselves, as reflected in Genesis 6:1, who are chained in darkness waiting for the Father's judgment, as referenced in Jude 1:6. The wall has no bearing on them. The second group are the one third of fallen angels that continue to serve Satan in whatever capacity he desires, and which is allowed by the Father. To them, the great wall that surrounds all of Heaven has significant meaning, as they are not permitted to enter anywhere."

This explained much to me, and I now think I understand its purpose. I thanked the Lord for His explanation.

Then I wanted to know if the Lord ever gets tired, and if so, where he goes to rest? I told Him I'd seen all kinds of fabulous mansions, so surely His must be over the top. Could He show it to me? He said yes, and He took me behind the Father's great throne to a one-room structure. In there was what appeared to be a simple single bed that was pushed up into one of the corners of the room. There in that room also stood a small table, maybe three feet square, all made out of wood. On the top of the table was what looked like a small lamp, like one that might use oil or kerosene, similar to what Jesus might have used for light when He needed it while He was still on the earth. I assumed that it was similar to the one He used as a boy growing up while he was on the earth. When I saw this room and the simple things in it, I was just stunned. It certainly wasn't what I expected for the King of Kings.

Then it was time for me to leave, so I thanked Him and said goodbye. Then I was back in the easy chair in my living room. All in all, it was a wonderful trip that lasted about twenty minutes.

Journey Number 27

DRIVEN BY THOUGHT AND
BILL'S JOURNEYS

O n Monday, September 10, 2018, shortly after ten in the morning. I was sitting in my easy chair when I heard His voice say, "Come on up." I still can't get over that the Creator of everything was speaking to me and inviting me to come to His house. It seemed like a good time for another trip.

I said, "In the name of Jesus, I call for the traveling angel to come and get me." In an instant, while my physical body stayed in the easy chair, my spirit body went out the front door and into the waiting chariot. Cyberin acknowledged me with a nod and smile. As we began to leave, I wondered, "Just what is it that powers this chariot?"

Without saying a word, Cyberin knew what I was thinking, and he began to laugh. "There are no motors pushing this, for it is driven by thought."

Did he just say a thought process powered the chariot? He laughed because, to him, the "thought process" is a common thing. He'd never known anything different. Now I was going back in time to other conversations we'd had, and I recalled being told that there are three methods of travel. Sound, light, and the fastest— thought. When Cyberin thought, the chariot did what he instructed by thought. It was just amazing.

All of this happened so fast, that by the time I realized it, we were already there, and I hadn't taken the time to just sit back and enjoy the spectacular view of space. As the chariot stopped in Heaven and I began to climb out, I looked around but didn't see anyone there. Cyberin waved goodbye, and off he and the chariot went. For a brief moment I just stood there looking.

Then I heard my name called. I instantly recognized the voice. It was my brother Bill. He came running up, and we embraced. "It's really good to see you again," he said.

He really looked good. I estimate that he was in his early thirties. He had black hair once again, and as before, it was in a small afro, and he still had his short, small, black mustache. "I've got so much to tell you and show you," he said.

We began to walk, and I got the feeling there was much he wanted to show me, because he started to pick up the pace. Obviously, he knew something I did not. All of sudden, he grabbed my arm and the two of us began to fly. Before long, we landed in front of a house. "This is my house," he was excited to say. "The Father knew I was coming and built this place just for me. Come on, I want to show you inside." Now I became very excited, since on all the previous trips I'd taken, I'd always been curious to see the inside of anyone of the mansions but was not allowed to. But here, with my brother Bill, I was now going to get to.

Bill's house didn't look like a huge mansion but a rather comfortable ranch house. As we stepped inside, I saw that the entrance room held a baby grand piano. Seeing it, the thought crossed my mind, "Does Bill play the piano here?" Then, turning to the left, I could see the great room. To my amazement, it was furnished with animal furniture. The coffee table was made out of an elephant ear, and the couch looked like it was out of zebra. Small tables at the end of the couch had deer legs where legs would normally be. There was a bear skin rug hanging on the wall and a lion skin rug on the floor.

"Are these real?" I asked.

He laughed. "No, but the Father knew I would really enjoy them, so He created these just to please me. Every time I look at them, I still can't believe it."

Bill took me into his kitchen. I couldn't believe my eyes. It appeared to look very similar to ones on the earth. Double sink with faucet, four-burner stove, oven, butcher-block center working station, cabinets, refrigerator, even what looked like a dishwasher. Hanging over the stove appeared to be a microwave.

As I stood there amazed, Bill laughed. "What's all this?" I said. "Surely you don't need all of this here in Heaven?"

"No," he said. "None of this is necessary. If we get hungry, there are amazing Heavenly foods we can eat. And if we want a certain thing, we just think it, and it appears. That's all there is to it. But remember that the Father has thought of all things for us. Therefore, if there comes a time when I get hungry for something from my past life, the Father has placed all of this here just in case I wanted to invite folks over and prepare for them what I felt like. So let's say I wanted to prepare a meal for you while you were here — say, duck. I just think duck, and it appears. I could wish it either done or raw, so I could prepare it for you. That would be my treat to you. Then, when the meal is over, everything cleans up on its own. I don't do anything, unless I want to. Pretty amazing isn't it?"

I was overwhelmed, but pleasantly surprised with this new information.

Bill had what he called a master bedroom, but I didn't see other bedrooms. He had a bed. It didn't appear to be a king size bed but maybe a queen size. He laughed as he told me that whenever he uses it, it remakes itself automatically. There were nightstands on each side, with lamps for reading, and a small sitting area off to the side by a door that led into a closet. I peered into his closet. There hanging, were several outfits of white, and down toward the end were different cloths, like the ones you would wear back on the earth. Shirts with different styles and colors and jeans, both in dark blue and black. As I looked at these, I simply had to ask, "Do you ever wear these?"

"I can whenever I want, but until now I just haven't wanted to."

Then he took me into the bathroom. I couldn't believe it. A bathroom in Heaven. There was a sink with a faucet similar to those on the earth, and a shower, but no toilet. I was curious. Bill told me there were times when he just felt like taking an underwater trip in one of the rivers or lakes, but because of what he was going to do next, the shower was more convenient for him at that moment. So was the sink.

Then I asked him that all important question. "What about the toilet?"

His answer revealed something I'd wondered about ever since I started taking these journeys. "Whatever we consume, regardless of whether it's heavenly food or something we desire from our past life, once we consume it, our bodies use everything, and we have no waste. That's true for both liquids and solid food. Our bodies here operate more perfectly than the ones we had on the earth.

I wanted to stay here in his home for a while longer, but I think he knew this trip was starting to come to an end, and he had one more thing he wanted me to see. We went back out the front door. He grabbed my left arm and, once again, we were flying. This time we headed toward the mountains.

Before I knew it, we arrived in a forested section of the mountains, where Bill was quickly met by a running squirrel, which was chirping as he ran toward Bill. Once he got to him, he ran up his left leg and continued up his back and onto his left shoulder. He continued to chirp into Bill's left ear. I could tell they knew each other, for Bill started speaking in strange sounds back to the squirrel. All the while, Bill was smiling like he had just found his long lost friend.

Soon the squirrel left, and I noticed Bill had spotted a deer not far from us. He motioned for me to come with him, and the two of us walked to the deer. Bill started stroking the side of his neck. It appeared as though the deer enjoyed it. Upon seeing this, I felt comfortable to do the same, and I was somewhat surprised that the deer just stood there and let me. As I was enjoying my encounter with the deer, Bill's attention was drawn to something else. He walked over to an elk that was standing not too far from us and just watching. All of a sudden, the elk bellowed as if he recognized Bill, and the two of them began walking toward each other. Once they met, Bill began to speak to the elk in a language I didn't understand. However, I was sure the elk did, as he kept raising and lowering his head. They stood there for quite a while, until another site caught Bill's eye, and in full stride, he ran toward it. As he ran, he was yelling at it. I looked, and I realized it was a black bear. Not a huge one. I estimated maybe three hundred pounds. When he saw Bill, he started running at him and growling. When they met, the bear tackled Bill, and they just rolled around in the grass for some time. It was apparent that this bear and Bill had known each other from previous encounters. It looked like it was a happy reunion between the two. I was just amazed as I watched my brother, who in a previous life used to love to hunt and kill these creatures. Now he was loving these friendship encounters. As the bear growled at Bill, Bill growled right back, and I realized they were communicating with each other. They wrestled in the grass for a while and then just stopped and sat next to each other, as old friends would often do. At one point it seemed like they were laughing together. Eventually the bear turned and started to walk away.

Bill just sat there for quite a while. He told me later that while he was just sitting there, he had to stop and thank the Father for allowing him to enjoy such an encounter. Eventually Bill walked back to where I was. To my amazement, Bill was not scratched or hurt anywhere, and the deer I had been stroking the neck of, had just stood by me and watched the encounter with Bill and the bear as well. It all seemed just so natural here.

Bill said it was time for me to leave, so the two of us flew back to where Cyberin and the chariot were waiting for me.

We said our goodbyes, and as I climbed into the chariot, I asked Bill what he did with most of his time. He told me he spent a lot of his time learning about the ways of the Father and his Son, Jesus. He said, "I just love spending time with Jesus." Then he added, "Do me a favor, Sam. Tell everyone you see you've seen me and that I was very much alive and doing just fine. Tell them this place is very, very real, and tell them to do everything they need to do to not miss coming here."

Then Cyberin and I were off and headed back to Earth. I just sat back and really enjoyed thinking about this encounter I'd just had with Bill and about the amazing scenery. When we landed, I thanked him for the ride and said goodbye. I walked back into the house, and there, waiting for me, was my physical body sitting in my easy chair. I was not sure this time just how long I was gone.

Journey Number 28

Prayer Warriors

O n Friday, September 20, 2018, I took my next journey; however, it affected me so much that I wasn't able to immediately write about it. It started around two in the afternoon. I had an idea that I would be taking a trip that afternoon but just didn't know when. That's when I heard His voice say, "Come on up." I had to make my way to a chair, settle in, and without saying a word, I just left. Instantly, there I was. I was now standing in Heaven. However, I found myself in an area of Heaven I'd never been before.

As I was looking around, a very large body of water appeared in front of me. It was a lake of sorts and quite large, for I was unable to see the other side, and the water was an amazing blue color. I didn't recall ever seeing this beautiful blue before. There were no waves, and I felt no breeze. The water was as flat as any body of water I'd ever seen. It was very beautiful to just stand and admire. I didn't see any boats or swimmers, nor did I hear any noise anywhere.

I turned around and notice a very large building. It looked like it was made of ivory. I know it wasn't, for I'd seen this material on other buildings here in Heaven before. I knew it was a heavenly material, but the closest thing I can compare to is ivory. While I was drawn to the beauty of the outside of this building, my curiosity was about what was happening on the inside.

As I walked up the two sets of steps, maybe twelve to fifteen steps each, I came to a very large double door. I estimate they were fifteen feet tall. However, as I approach and began looking at the massive size of the doors, I wonder whether I would be able to open them. Before I could take a hold of one of the door handles, to my amazement, both doors opened by themselves. So, I just walked in.

I was now inside of the entrance of a very large corridor. In the past, when I approached other buildings here in Heaven, I could hear voices, singing, or musical instruments being played. That is not the case here. It was strangely very quiet in the corridor. I saw several doors that led to the inside. In fact, I was standing very close to one of central ones. I decide to enter, and I grabbed hold of the door handle and began to open it to see what was on the inside.

As I walked inside, first I was awestruck by the enormity of the interior. It was one huge hall — at least four to five hundred feet wide and thousands of feet deep. I saw saints along with angels everywhere. There must have been thousands and thousands, possibly millions of them. I was curious. What were they all doing here? I was amazed to see they were all praying. Some were sitting on chairs at tables, while others were standing. Some were walking around, and others were just lying flat on the floor.

I took a few steps inside, and my knees began to buckle under the weight of the glory of God that was in this building. It was so thick that I felt I could cut it with a knife, for I literally felt some of the weight of this intense glory, while at the same time I was consumed in it, and I couldn't help but praise and worship the Heavenly Father, His Son, Jesus, and the precious Holy Spirit, the Spirit of God.

Some time went by. I was not sure how long, but eventually I began to look around again. I noticed some were praying out loud, while others were silently praying. I wondered who all these were and what their specific purpose here was.

Then the Lord told me that these were Heaven's "prayer warriors." Just as everyone on the earth was given at least one gift from the Father that they could have used while they were there, the gift they have here always corresponds with their individual task here in Heaven. These, then, were the heavenly prayer warriors, whose job it was to prayer for the saints still alive on the earth, as well as those on the earth who will accept God's free gift of his Son and become saved through faith in Jesus Christ.

Then the Lord told me that the angels were praying not only for those still on the earth but for their fellow angels that are doing battle with the enemy, as they are sent from Heaven to bring answers to prayers to those on the earth. He told me that He had several of these prayer warrior buildings in various places throughout Heaven.

I was not sure how long I stayed in the building. I do know that I didn't want to leave, but I felt as though I could not have stayed much longer under the weight of the glory of God. It is an overwhelming presence.

Soon it was time for me to leave, and once again, I found myself back in my physical body and in the easy chair back in the living room.

Journey Number 29

THE BEAUTY OF THE COSMOS & MEETING MARY

At 9:14 p.m. on Sunday, October 7, 2018, Cyberin picked me up. I'd felt earlier in the day that sometime soon I would be traveling on another trip, so it was not a surprise when he arrived. As I sat in the chariot, I assumed the traveling would be pretty much the same as before, but as we traveled away from the earth into outer space, Cyberin suddenly stopped the chariot, or at least it appeared that he had stopped. I wasn't sure whether you really stop when traveling in space, because in space, there are no reference points to confirm one way or the other if you are really standing still. It appeared as though we had stopped for a brief moment. I was able to stand up and look around at the magnificent beauty of space.

First, the stars in the cosmos are so many that there is absolutely no human way that they could be numbered. As I stood there taking them in, I was reminded that God named them all and knows each and every one of His creations, but the beauty and brilliance of these, well, there just are no adequate words to describe them. The colors—bright white, vibrant red, yellow gold, and emerald green— stuck out to me so much as I was looking at them. I was amazed that, as I looked at them, they were also both to my left and right. In addition, as I looked up and behind me, I was overwhelmed to see them there also, and even below me. They were everywhere. It was as though I was in the center of them, for they were all around. Cyberin must have known how much I would enjoy seeing this, for we seemed to stay there for a little while. I was overtaken by the beauty of it all and continued to marvel at its beauty and the handy work by the Creator of this magnificent masterpiece.

Once again, we began to journey, and as we became closer to Heaven, it seemed like Heaven was in the center or crossroads of all of space, but I was not sure if this is accurate. I wondered if it was possible, given all of the stars, planets, and galaxies, if in all of the Master's creation, He'd decided to place His home in the center of it all. As we were approaching Heaven, yet still some distance away, I could see that it is lit up from within with the brightest light. As we came closer, it was stunning to look at, with its great wall surrounding it and Paradise sitting adjacent to it.

Soon, we landed in Heaven at a familiar place, and as I exited the chariot, again Cyberin nodded his goodbye with a big smile and his usual wave from his right hand. At the same time, Abraham came walking toward me. "Hello Sam," he said, and his greeting was comforting to me. We engaged in a bear hug. "It's good to see you again," he said. "I'm here to take you to see someone very special. You're really going to enjoy meeting with them."

Soon we were off walking. I could tell he was excited to introduce me to this person, for I could tell that he was struggling to hold back the introduction, so we just continued to walk for a little while.

He told me he'd noticed that there had been an increase of excitement from those already here about those that were preparing to come there. So he was curious about current events going on the earth. We spoke briefly about it, as the walk was not too far.

As we turned the corner, I saw who he had brought me here to see. There she was. It was Mary, the mother of Jesus. She was just sitting on a bench, just waiting for me. When Abraham greeted Mary, it was obvious they had known each other for some time.

Then he introduced me to Mary. She didn't get up, and I asked her if we could talk.

"Sure," she said, and she motioned for me to come and sit down with her on the bench. When I did, she gave me a welcomed hug and said, "I've been expecting you." I was still puzzled. How did she know I was coming? Abraham didn't say a thing, but just started to walk away. I guess his job for the moment was done.

Like others there, Mary appeared to be in her early thirties. The first thing that caught me was her eyes. They were large and a very stunning black. You could not help but notice them. She had long, jet-black hair, which ran well below her shoulders. Then I noticed her skin, which was almost olive in color. She was very beautiful. Admiring her beauty, I began wondering about her personality. In other words, was she as beautiful on the inside as she was on the outside?

"Do you remember much about your life on the earth?" I asked.

"Yes, almost all of it," she said.

I asked her if she could remember from the beginning when she was visited by the angel Gabriel. She smiled and said that Gabriel and she had become quite good friends here.

Then she said, "When I was growing up, until that visit, I never thought I was anybody special. However, when the angel Gabriel first approached me and called me highly favored by God, I was shocked to say the least, because he hadn't yet revealed the Father's plan to me. In addition, having this awesome angel standing there in front of me was extremely overwhelming.

"When He told me I was going to become pregnant without me ever knowing a man, but that the Spirit of Father God would come to me to do the job, well at first I tried to figure out just how it would all happen and understand how that would work. But you must understand that I was standing here in front of a Heavenly angel sent by God, who told me he'd just been standing in the presence of God and was given this message to give to me. In addition, he told me that the child I would give birth to would one day rule over all of Israel and that when his kingdom was established, it would last forever. This was too big for me to doubt, so I just accepted it.

"For the first several months of the pregnancy, I chose to hide myself from neighbors, relatives, and friends. Then I heard about Zacharias's wife Elizabeth being pregnant. She was quite up in years, so I decided to go and see her to see how she was getting along. When I saw her, I realized that her pregnancy like mine, was also a miracle.

"The birth of my son, Jesus, was very special, in spite of where He was born. Angels were everywhere celebrating His birth. It was then that John and I both realized just who He was, and that made both of us extremely humbled, yet thrilled.

By the time Jesus was thirty, I was anxious to see Him as the ruler of everything. I actually thought that one day soon He could be king over all of Israel. I knew He'd been sent by God, and that's why, when we went to the wedding feast in Cana, I thought He could help with the wine problem. It was so simple for Him, and it made the celebration even more enjoyable.

"However, when they arrested Him and put him on the cross, my heart sank, as I watched my Son, the gift from God, give up His spirit and die. After they had placed His body in the tomb, since He wasn't properly prepared for burial, I went with others to place spices and perfume on his body. We were talking about how we were going to get the stone removed so we could go in. However, what a glorious sight it was when we saw that the tomb was empty and the angel told us He was not there, for He had risen, just as He had said He would. I ran with the others to tell the other disciples.

What a thrill it was for all of us there in the upper room as Jesus appeared to us. I was full of joy as my Son, the Savior of the world, had been resurrected, just like He said He would. The days that He spent with us after that were filled with such joy. He continued to teach and prepare many for their mission. Seeing Him in full swing was the ultimate joy for any mother, and I am so blessed that the Father elected me to be His Son's mother, for His story swept all over the country as His disciples introduced people to the Father's gift.

"Now, I am overjoyed here, as everyone knows who He is and that I am His mother."

Next, I wanted to find out about some of the things she'd been doing while in Heaven.

"Oh," she said, "without a doubt, my favorite thing to do is visit with Jesus. Looking at the King of Kings, it's hard to realize it wasn't too long ago that he was living inside of me. Now it brings me such joy when I think about the fact that I was a part of God's plan for all of mankind. When I sit down with Jesus and look at His hands and feet, and realize who He is, I really enjoy spending time with Him.

"Also, I was seeing and spending time with my other children. You know, at first they didn't believe who Jesus was. Now everybody here knows Him, and we all look forward to seeing Him where He comes around. We have ongoing conversations about Him. Everyone here realizes who He is, and we all enjoy having conversations with Him and about Him. In addition, all of us here have been given an assignment to continually pray for those that are still alive on the earth, that they will also recognize who He is and eventually arrive here when it is their time."

It was time for me to leave, so I thanked Mary for her time and said I'd like to come back and sit down with her some more. She said she would like that also. After we said our goodbyes, back to Cyberin and the chariot I went. Soon I was back in my physical body in the easy chair in the living room. It was now 9:41 p.m. I had been gone for twenty-seven minutes. Reflecting on my time with Mary, I just have to say that she is a very nice person.

Journey Number 30

QUESTIONS FROM THE
HEAVENLY SAINTS

O n Sunday, November 5, 2018, I returned from a wonderful trip that lasted just over one hour. It started at 3:17 p.m. I heard the Lord say to me, "Are you ready?"

"Yes," I said. "And in the name of Jesus, I call for the traveling angel to come and pick me up." Up out of the easy chair my spirit body went and out the front door. As usual, there in the front yard, waiting on me was Cyberin, sitting in the front of the chariot. He had a huge grin on his face. For a brief moment, I stood by the front door of the house while I attempted to study the chariot and its driver.

The first thing that I noticed was the cloud or mist that the chariot was hovering in. Because of it, I couldn't see the whole picture of the chariot. I could only see its upper portion, which, of course, included Cyberin. I could see that He was all dressed in white and had slightly tan colored or light golden hair that ran down to just below his shoulders. It was also wavy or slightly curly. The portion of the chariot I could see was covered in a brilliant red and had gold leaf all throughout. It was very impressive.

I climbed into the rear seat. Cyberin always sat in the front. In all my trips, I never did. There were no seat belts or harnesses. Nothing was needed to hold you in. He turned to see that I was in position, and off we went. I was once again mesmerized by the beauty of the colors of the earth, with its various shades of green, blues, white, and different shades of brown, from light to dark. Of all of the planets I'd been privileged to see, without a doubt, I think Earth is the most beautiful, especially when seen from a distance.

Once again, there we were in outer space, traveling at an amazing speed. Yet, it was not so fast that it was all a blur. On the contrary, the beauty of space is a sight to behold, with its millions and millions of stars in all colors, its planets, not to mention galaxies.

Before we knew it, we were there. Just to think of it—Heaven! Wow, what a beautiful place. It does't matter where you land, it's all so wonderful, and I was glad to be back. But Cyberin took me to a new place.

Before he brought the chariot to a complete stop, I noticed a large group of people waiting for me, and as I got out of the chariot and thanked Cyberin for the ride, this substantial group of individuals proceeded to gather around me. I estimated that there were at least sixty to seventy-five there. Since this was a completely different area from where I had ever been before, and as we had not been together before, I surmised that they must have heard from other people there in Heaven about my journeys back and forth from the earth to Heaven.

Not only were they curious to see who I was, but as I started to encounter them, I realized they had lots and lots of questions. Some greeted me with smiles, some with hugs, some just took my hand for a good heavenly handshake.

Then the questions started. What's it like to travel back and forth? I told them that the Father usually provided a chariot and an angelic driver, so I'd been able to sit back and enjoy the wonderful view of parts of the cosmos, with its awesome beauty. I spoke to them about the Father teaching me to call for the chariot and driver in the name of Jesus. I said this method had worked every time. I also told them that, at times, the Spirit of God just reached down from Heaven and pulled me there in just an instant. I spoke about the different speeds at which Cyberin had driven the chariot, and therefore, at times I just felt that we just left, and then we were there, while at other times he seemed to take his time so that I could enjoy the awesome views. Since no one I spoke with had enjoyed this part of my journeys, I tried to explain these parts of some of my journeys, but as yet, I found it really hard to come up with adequate words to describe this for them, especially the wonderful views of the cosmos. None of those I spoke with had indicated they'd had this wonderful experience.

Next, we talked about traveling at the speed of light and traveling by thought. Some confirmed that they had learned to travel one of these ways. It became clear that most used thought, as that was the mode that most were taught here.

Next, the questions regarding those current issues that were currently going on the earth started, as well as some items I had known about from history. I was really surprised to hear people speak of plans that had been executed here in Heaven that did affect outcomes of historical events on the earth.

But without a doubt, the two greatest areas of conversation concerned the nation of Israel and the progression and growth of the church. Some were not informed that the nation of Israel had become a reborn nation in 1948, and of course, there was much discussion about the fulfillment of the Word, which, by the way is very much alive in Heaven. We talked about the scattering of the people of Israel and the returning, as described in Ezekiel 36 and 37. All of the people I spoke with here had not been born prior to the beginning of the nineteenth century. Therefore, the only things they knew about the movement or growth of the church was what they could remember or had been told by those coming to Heaven since they were there.

I tried to explain to them about the electronic age, television, computers, laptops, and satellites. I could tell that much of what I was telling them was going over their heads. But they certainly understood and became very excited as they realized that these were all tools being used in this age to get the Gospel out to places all over the world that had never been allowed before. I explained that there still were places in the world that refused to allow ministers, missionaries, and written Gospel material into their countries, but they couldn't stop the airways, no matter how hard they tried. So the Gospel is being preached to people all over the world all at the same time, with the result that millions and millions of people were able to hear the story of Jesus each and every day, and as a result, millions and millions were accepting Christ as their Savior. People started praising the Lord, and before I realized it, we were all caught up in the worship of the King.

There was so much I wanted to ask about Heaven, but I knew that the time was drawing near for me to return back to earth, so they told me that the next time we were together, they world answer my questions first. They thanked me for my time, and I noticed Cyberin and the chariot waiting, so I walked over to it, and as I climbed into the chariot, we said a heavenly goodbye, and off we went.

Before long we were back in the front yard. Cyberin smiled, waved goodbye, and he was off. Then I went back inside the house to my body, just waiting for me as it was when I left. It was now 4:22 p.m. I had been gone just over an hour.

Journey Number 31

PERSONAL VISIT WITH
THE LORD

O n Saturday, November 17, 2018, my trip started at 1:32 p.m. and lasted until 2:07 p.m. I was gone for over half an hour. I heard the Master's voice say, "Come up here," and instantly I was there. I didn't call for the traveling angel, and no chariot came for me. One minute, I was here, and then the next second, I was there.

Instantly I was in the presence of Jesus. When I saw Him, I immediately fell to the floor in worship. As He helped me to my feet, I noticed His wonderful and loving smile.

For the first time, we hugged, and I felt so all at home and at peace with Him. I had been carrying around three very personal questions that I wanted to ask Him the next time that we met, so this was my opportunity. Because these were personal, I have not included any of them here—neither my questions to Him nor His answers.

Needless to say, my trip was not very long, and I didn't see anything else, or anybody else. I just returned after about thirty minutes with the Lord, with my questions answered.

Journey Number 32

RACHEL AND MARY

O n Friday, November 30, 2018, I took another journey, although I was not sure how long I was gone, as I didn't look at the clock before I left. I'm estimating that I was gone around forty-five minutes to an hour.

For a couple of days prior to that day, I knew I would be taking a journey today. So when the time was right, I just settled into my easy chair and said, "In the name of Jesus, I call for the traveling angel to come and pick me up." However, my trip there didn't last as long as some of the previous ones, and before I knew it, I was there.

To my surprise, and a pleasant surprise it was, only one person was there to greet me. It was my daughter, Rachel, and she was just standing there waiting for me. I asked her how she knew I was coming and where we would be landing. She said, "We just know."

Rachel and I embraced and gave each other a hello kiss. Then Rachel said, "Hi Daddy." This, as usual, just melted my heart. She was such a pretty woman, with her dark brown, shoulder-length hair and her mother's hazel eyes. Ever since we met the very first time, I'd often wondered what she did during her daily activities. I also wanted to know where she lived and who she spent her time with. These were the kinds of things that a father would want to know.

We began to walk, and she put her left arm in mine and told me we weren't very far from her home, so she wanted to take me there to show it to me. Before long, we were standing in front of it. It was a small bungalow. It was cute, but I could tell it was not very big. However, she told me she just loved it, especially seeing that her Heavenly Father made it just for her. Once inside, and after looking around, I estimated that it was maybe eight or nine hundred square feet. The place was very well decorated and had quite a warm, comfortable feeling about it. I could tell Rachel loved plants, as they were everywhere. Some were flowers with colors I had never seen before. They were just beautiful.

As we sat down inside, I asked what kind of activities she engaged in. She told me she meet with others on a daily basis to study God's Word. Then she surprised me when she told me that one of her favorite things to do was meet with five or six others to study the Word, with her Grandpa Radobenko as the leader for the group. The group she was studying with were just like her and had never lived on the earth; therefore, studying events that happened on the earth was very intriguing to them. She said they had such a good time together as they listen to Grandpa tell various Bible stories then mixed some of them up with actual history.

Then she told me she had someone that I'd met before that wanted to see me again. She wouldn't tell me who it was, because she wanted it to be a surprise.

We left her cute little bungalow. As we walked, she said something quite interesting to me. "You know, Dad, I'll never know a man as a husband." That statement caught me off guard. Then she said, "But that's okay, because Jesus is my husband, and I can't imagine love there on the earth with an earthly husband being any greater than it is here. Here, the Father's love is so great, you're always full."

As we continued to walk, I began to recognize a few familiar sights. Then we came around the corner, and there she was, just sitting on a bench, just like before. It was Mary, the mother of Jesus, and she was just waiting for me. It was obvious that Mary and Rachel knew each other well. In fact, after listening to them talk with each other, I was convinced they were good friends. Mary must have had a previous conversation with Rachel and told her that when she saw me the next time, to bring me by so we could talk again.

Upon seeing the two of them together, my first thought was that Mary had lived well over two thousand years ago, while Rachel, had she been born, would have been less than fifty years old. Yet, here, they both looked the same age, in their early thirties.

After Mary and I greeted each other, she motioned for me to have a seat with her on the bench. She told me that she'd been praying for me. For some reason, she wanted me to know that. Kiddingly, I thanked her and told her I needed all of the prayers I could get. But to my amazement, she was not kidding, and I realized she took prayer very seriously. I realized my lighthearted response was inappropriate.

Mary wanted to know if I'd been enjoying the trips. I tried to describe the beauty the entire cosmos had, with its brilliant colors, but I felt as if I fell short in describing such a wonder, just like I previously had as I had tried to do that with some while on the earth. Next, she wanted to know about things that were going on the earth, like the growth of the church and her people in Israel. I remember that we had briefly spoken about both of these the last time that we'd seen each other. She appeared to get very excited as we talked first about the church and how it had grown to cover the world, with million and millions every few days now accepting Jesus as their personal Savior.

Trying to tell someone about new technology, when all they knew growing up was a donkey or traveling on foot, puzzled me, because now Mary could travel by light, or even better, by thought. Yet, she wanted to know how it was all possible to reach the entire world with the salvation message. I attempted to talk to her about radio, then television, followed by satellites, dish technology, and cell phones. Then I explained that we were in the age of tech-nology. It was interesting to see her and Rachel light up as they both realized that right now, we were fulfilling the prophecy in Daniel, chapter twelve.

Then we spoke about her people, the nation of Israel. She told me she knew the nation was in trouble while she was alive. I explained to her that, because of their sin, God had scattered them all over the world, and for over two thousand years, the land of Israel stood desolate, with no one living there. However, God had said He would bring them back again, and in 1948, once again, Israel became a nation. Since that time, even though they'd endured great opposition, they hadn't only survived but had become a major country in that region of the world.

As I continued to visit with Mary, it became obvious that she was studying me for some reason. Before I could ask her why, she told me she was still very curious as to why I was allowed to go back and forth on these trips. She wanted to see what made me so special. I just smiled and told her I'd just asked the Father if I could. I thought that when He said yes, it was too easy, until I came and met with her Son, Jesus, who told me it became an assignment from the Father so that what I would learn from those there, and what I would see when there, I could then put into writing, and as others would read it, then they would become encouraged. I said it really had nothing to do with me. I was no one special, and the Father could have used just anyone.

Then it was time for me to leave. I thanked Mary for her time, and as we hugged goodbye, she looked me directly in the eye and said she would be continually praying for me as I carried out this task for the Father. I thanked her, and Rachel, and I headed back to where we had first met. On the way back, she told me the two of them meet quite frequently, and they had become good friends. She said that when they got together, they were always praying for me. I was overwhelmed with this thought.

Once we arrived at my departure destination, there was Cyberin, just sitting and waiting in the chariot. As Rachael and I embraced and kissed goodbye, she told me to say hi to her mom and brother, and then we were off.

I just sat back and enjoyed the ride. At some point along the way, Cyberin asked me if I had enjoyed the trip. I told him that I really enjoyed visiting with my daughter, as well as Mary. He said that before he had picked me up, he knew who I would be visiting with, so he knew I would really enjoy this trip.

We landed in the front yard, and I exited the chariot. Cyberin smiled and waved goodbye, and in an instant, he was gone. I entered the house, and there in the living room, waiting for me, was my body, just sitting in the easy chair, just like it was when I left. I was not sure how long I'd gone, but comparing it with other trips, it seemed like forty-five minutes to an hour.

Journey Number 33

ABRAHAM WITH DAD AT HIS HOME

O n Thursday, December 27, 2018, I began another journey. When I heard His voice say, "Come up here," I glanced at the clock. It was 3:07 p.m. I was gone for twenty minutes this time.

It all started when I said, "In the name of Jesus I call for the traveling angel to come and pick me up." When my spirit body went out the front door, I saw Cyberin waiting. When he saw me, he gave me a wave with his right hand, and a smile was all over his face. I got the impression he was glad to see me. I climbed into the chariot, and off we went.

It wasn't long before we were in outer space. I found myself mesmerized by the beauty of space, with its various planets, and clusters of stars just gleaming with all sorts of beautiful colors. I had always thought that stars were just white, but I was so wrong. There are brilliant and different shades of reds, orange, yellows, not to mention the emerald greens, as well as colors I had never seen before, all mixed together, making this journey just a wonder to behold. I just sat back and enjoyed the ride. However, at some point along the way, it looked like there was a crossroads in Heaven, kind of like the center of it all, and right in the middle of it, was an enormously bright white light. That's exactly where Cyberin took us in the chariot.

As we landed and I began to climb out of the chariot, I heard a familiar voice. All of my conversations with Cyberin were telepathic. However, this one that I was hearing was not. It was audible. "Hello," he said, and as I turned around to see who it was, I recognized the person walking toward me. It was Abraham.

"How are you, Sam" he said. "It's good to see you again. Come with me. We have special people to see.

As we started to walk away, I turned to thank Cyberin for the enjoyable ride. Again, he waved and, with the same smile on his face, he was off. So now it was just me and Abraham. I still couldn't get over his size. He was at least six foot four, and a very barrel-chested man. I felt he could lead everyone to do anything that needed doing. He was that kind of guy.

"Abraham," I said, "I have a question. Why did God create all of the stars and planets? I mean, as humans, it's impossible for man to enjoy all of the beauty that the heavens behold. So why did He create them? Did He have another purpose in doing so?"

His answer caught me off guard. "The Father originally created them for His angels to enjoy. You see, when they were created, no humans existed. Therefore, any of the angels could leave Heaven and travel out into space and marvel at the work of the Father's hands. In fact, they were also allowed to travel great distances to other planets. That's the way it was originally. Except for Enoch and Elijah, only after Jesus completed His resurrection and came back to Heaven were humans introduced into Heaven. Now, just like the angels, they can travel into space to enjoy the wonderful scenery, all the while praising the Father for His handiwork, and they can now travel to those planets to see what they are like too."

I was just blown away by what he is telling me. I got the feeling we had a scheduled appointment or appointments, which he didn't want us to be late for, because before I knew it, he reached over and grabbed my left wrist, and we began flying.

I wondered where we were going that was so important. I knew the different types of traveling here: one, as fast as lightning; two, the speed of sound; and three, the fastest, by speed of thought. But before I realized it, we were at our first destination, and we were standing out in the front of a very large multistory mansion. I was blown away by the manicured front lawn. It was just pristine, with not a blade of grass out of place. The lawn was manicured to perfection, with edges that looked like they'd been trimmed by hand with a pair of scissors. Then I noticed that the walkway up to the house was lined with tulips in full bloom and all in straight rows. All of the bushes up by the house were perfectly trimmed and in full bloom, and I began to wonder just whose house this was. Then I saw him standing on the front porch. It was my dad, and this was the house that the Father had prepared just for him, the way he liked.

As Abraham and I walked up to him, we greet each other with a hug, and he said to me, "It's good to see you again Sam." He also acknowledged Abraham, and they embraced. He had a big grin on his face, and I was not sure if he was glad to see me or just wanted to show me his place.

I asked him if I could look inside, and he nodded. I opened the front door to a grand entrance area, which I estimated to be the size of many small houses back on the earth. There were two sets of stairs, one on each side, going up to the next level. It was all just breathtaking. Then I looked straight ahead, down the hall, which looked like it went on forever. I was just blown away by all of this.

My dad was just grinning ear to ear, and he said, "This is what the Father designed and built for me. Isn't it wonderful?"

I was now speechless. It was just amazing. This mansion must have been at least twenty thousand square feet.

Abraham said we must leave because we had another appointment, but I told him that we just got here. But it was no use, so we said goodbye.

Dad said, "Be sure to tell that women that bore my children that I love her and miss her, and I am looking forward to seeing her with me here very soon." Also, please tell Donna that I love her too."

Then Abraham grabbed my left wrist again and we flew away from Dad and his home. I turned and saw Dad waving goodbye. "See you again soon, son. Keep up the good work, and remember I'm praying for you."

Before long, we were landing in front of two identical houses right next to each other. Both of my in-laws, Merle and Betty, were sitting on one of the porches, just waiting for me. These were not huge mansions, like my father's. I estimated they were three thousand five hundred to four thousand square feet each, both single level and very comfortable looking. Just like at my father's place, the front yard was impeccable, with its grass, flowers, and landscaping, but you couldn't tell where one property ended and the other started. It was as though they were joined together at the hip and designed that way from the beginning. These were not duplexes but individual houses sitting right next to each other.

As Abraham and I began to walk to the porch, both of my in-laws stood up with big grins on their faces and gave both Abraham and me a very warm hug. Obviously, they were both well acquainted with Abraham. I was sure he was well loved by everyone here, and it just goes without saying that they were glad to see me again.

"How have the trips been going," said Merle. "We've been aware of your journeys back and forth but wanted to hear firsthand from you."

We spoke briefly about a few of my past experiences. I particularly wanted to tell them about seeing Rachel again. They were aware of it because, after that trip, Rachel had come to see them and tell them all about it. I was quite pleased to hear that they were seeing each other and had already discussed it together.

I mentioned that I had noticed the two houses and was informed that the Father had designed and built one for each of them, but He knew how much they loved each other, so He put them right next to each other. I said they looked so similar on the outside and was told that that's where the similarity stopped. Each house was very

Abraham With Dad At His Home

different on the inside. Merle's was more masculine; Betty's had a more feminine theme. The porch of the house we were standing in was Merle's.

I wanted to go inside and see the differences, but Abraham indicated that I would have to do that on another trip because we were running out of time and would have to leave very soon.

My father-in-law then said, "Be sure to tell the girls when you see them that you have seen us and that we love them and are praying for them, and tell Sammy too.

We said our goodbyes, and Abraham and I flew back to where we'd met. Cyberin and the chariot were just waiting for us. I shook hands with Abraham and thanked him for the journey. Then we were off, and I just sat back in the chariot to enjoy the picturesque ride while reflecting on the journey's encounters.

Upon landing in the front yard, I thanked Cyberin for the ride, and with his usual grin on his face he waved goodbye, and off he went. I went back inside the house to my waiting body, just sitting in the easy chair. As I sat in the chair, I looked at the clock. It was now 3:27 p.m. I'd been gone a fully packed twenty minutes.

Journey Number 34

HE DIDN'T FORGET ME, PEARL

O n Tuesday, January 22, 2019, at three fifteen in the morning, I took a short nineteen minute journey. As I was sitting in my easy chair, I spoke those usual traveling words. "In the name of Jesus, I call the traveling angel to come and pick me up." Then my spirit body left my physical body in the chair and hurried out the front door. I was trying to get into the front yard before Cyberin got there. However, as hurried as I was, I did not do it. He was just sitting in the chariot in the front yard, ready and waiting, with his big grin on his face, and his hello wave. I climbed into the chariot and sat back, expecting to enjoy the usual picturesque ride. However, Cyberin must have been instructed otherwise, for before I knew it, we were already there. That certainly was a fast ride.

We didn't land in our usual spot, and I didn't recognize where we were. I had not been at this spot before. As I climbed out of the chariot, I realized we were on the top of a short bluff slightly outside of the city.

Cyberin left, and I expected someone to be standing there in this strange place to meet me. Since no one was there, I decided to start walking down the short hill. That's when I heard a familiar voice call my name. However, when I say a familiar voice, I don't mean familiar to me as one of those I had previously met in one of my previous journeys. Instead, it was one I recognized from my time on the earth, and as I continued to walk down the hill, there she was, walking up the hill to meet me.

At first, she was too far away to actually see who she was, but I certainly recognized her voice. It was Pearl, the mother of one of my closest friends. Less than two months earlier, at ninety-six years young, the Lord had called her to be with Him. Yet, as we embraced, there she was in front of me, not as a woman in her nineties but a beautiful woman in her prime, which I would estimate to be in her early thirties. Her face was just radiant with the glory of the Father. She just looked stunning. She had a smile on her face that went ear to ear and was so infectious.

"You told me He hadn't forgotten me, and you were right Sam, for I'm here with Him in this wonderful place."

I wanted to ask her if she remembered those last few breaths she'd taken on the earth, what happened then, and who met her once she arrived. I had so many questions. I also wanted to know what it was like for her when she first met Jesus.

"He was the first person I met when I arrived. An angel came into my room, and we went fast as lightning to Heaven. As soon as I realized what had happened, Jesus was standing in front of me. When I realized who it was, I bowed my face all the way to the ground. He called me by my first name and helped me to my feet. Then he extended His open arms to welcome me. I looked into His eyes. He has the most gorgeous eyes, and yet I felt that, as He was looking at me, He could look right through me, all the way to my soul. Then He spoke. I still can't get over what He said to me. He said, 'Welcome, welcome, my faithful child. I'm so glad you are here with me now. You accomplished much for me while you were on the earth. I have many rewards for you here.'

"And yet, as I stood there in front of Him, even though I thought I was still in my old body, I wasn't, and as I looked at my arms and legs, I was looking at the limbs of a young person. I couldn't believe it was me. I couldn't believe it. I was young again! I had beautiful hair and no wrinkles. As I said that, Jesus began to laugh. He said, 'I have so much more in store for you. I'm excited for you to experience it. Now I have to go, but we will meet from time to time. I have others here that I want you to see. We'll talk again soon.'

"As He started to walk away, here came my mom and dad. What a wonderful reunion we had. It was interesting—they didn't look like they did their last days on the earth—old and worn out. They looked young and vibrant, just like I do. In fact, they looked the same age as me. However, I was still able to recognize them and they me."

I wanted to know how that was possible. Not knowing how much time I was going to have on this trip, I had to know more. I asked who else she'd met since she'd been there.

"Let's see," she said. "There was Eck; your dad; Merle and Betty; Mary, the Mother of Jesus; and your daughter Rachael, just to name a few. By the way, she certainly is a beautiful woman."

Before I knew it, Cyberin was there, just standing by the chariot, waiting. That told me it was time to leave. I told Pearl I had to go.

"So soon?" she said. "It seems like you just got here. Be sure and tell my son that I love him, and Eric, Tina, and the great grandkids also, and I'm looking forward to seeing all of them here with me soon."

We hugged and said goodbye. As she turned around and started walking down the hill, I heard her say, "Weeeeeee! Weeeeeeeee!"

My head was full as I climbed into the chariot, and I think Cyberin knew it, for he didn't say a word all the way home. He just smiled, as if to say, "Mission accomplished."

Then I found myself sitting in my physical body in the easy chair, engulfed in the goodness of all that I had just experienced. Praise the Lord!

Journey Number 35

THE PRECIOUS REUNION

O n Thursday, March 7, 2019, I was sitting in my easy chair in the living room when I heard Him speak gently to me. "It's time," He said. I decided that rather than sitting in the chair to call for my chariot and driver, in an effort to beat him to the front yard, I would get up, and as I quickly walked through the living room, I said, "In the name of Jesus, I call for the traveling angel and chariot to come and pick me up."

Through the front door I went, and to my surprise, Cyberin arrived to meet me. This was the first time that I was able to see the chariot arrive. Always in the past, whenever I went through the front door, the chariot and driver were already there, so it was interesting to see them arrive. As always, Cyberin had his usual big grin on his face. As I headed toward the chariot, I acknowledged Cyberin, climbed into the chariot, and sat down.

Without a moment's hesitation, we were off. But instead of heading straight into outer space, we climbed to a certain height, and Cyberin began to circle the earth. I guess it was so that I could enjoy the scenery from where we were. I assumed we must have been hundreds of miles into space, because I was able to make out geographical locations on the earth like places on the map—countries and certain bodies of water. What really struck me were the different colors of the earth at different locations. There were light and dark browns, for instance, and several shades of green and blues, not to mention reds and white. The earth is a very colorful place. Cyberin must have also enjoyed its wonders, as He took us around the globe not once but two times before He headed out and in the direction of Heaven.

On the outskirts of Heaven sits Paradise. It has been there for over two thousand years, ever since Jesus rose from the grave. One could walk between Paradise and the gates into Heaven. Since the glory of God fills all of Heaven, the job of some saints there was to train children along with new converts who arrive in Paradise before they can become familiar with God's glory. So as Cyberin and I were heading into Heaven, we passed through a portion of Paradise. I was surprised to see saints waving at us and smiling as we went by. Of course we waved back to them. I was not sure if they knew who we were or what we were doing or whether seeing a chariot in air was a familiar thing to them. Anyway, I enjoyed them waving to us, and I smiled and waved back to them.

As we arrived at our usual destination, I noticed a substantial gathering there waiting for us. Before I exited the chariot, I recognized several people there. My dad and my brother Bill were there, along with my in-laws, Merle and Betty. I also noticed my daughter Rachel, my grandmother, my mother's mother, along with two close friends, Paula R. and Pearl E. Eventually, in addition, I also recognized Mary, the Mother of Jesus.

Dad and I were the first to embrace. He said, "It's good to see you again, son. You're looking good for making all of these trips. We were just discussing how all these trips could have a toll on you, but it looks like you're handling it well. Are you enjoying coming and going, and the scenery? Tell me, what do you think of this place? Do you know how many more times you'll be traveling here and then going back?"

Before I could begin to answer, my brother Bill spoke next. "Sam," he said. "Can you come and spend some time with me this trip? There are a lot more things that I want to show you that I've learned about since the last time you were here and we went to the mountains together."

I said I didn't usually know in advance what I'd be seeing or who. So each trip was always a surprise to me. "So, we'll have to see, but I'd sure like to," I told him. He wasn't disappointed and said that he understood.

Paula was next to speak. As we embraced, I told her she looked the best I'd ever seen her. She just laughed and said, "Thank you, but everyone here looks their best because we are continually basking in the glory of God. You just can't help it. By the way, I have a message for my husband Paul that I'd like you to tell him for me, if you can. Please tell him I love him and that I'm praying for him."

I told her that I was fairly confident the Father wouldn't mind me doing that, so I assured her that the next time I spoke with Paul, I'd give him her message and that I was sure he would enjoy hearing it.

As I looked around, I could not help but notice the big smile on my father-in-law, Merle's, face. On Earth, he was not a big hugger, but without hesitation we embraced. I said hello to him, then I also hugged my mother-in-law, Betty. Once again, I couldn't get over how good they both looked, and I said so. They just smiled and said, "Thank you."

I looked to my right and saw my grandmother, my mom's mother. "Hi, Grandma," I said, and we hugged. She looked so radiant, and she had a wonderful glow about her. Her long dark hair just glistened.

"It's good to see you again, Sammy," she said. "When you can, I'd like to sit down with you and just talk. The Father has been so good to me to just let me be here. If not on this trip, maybe the next time that you come." I was delighted to hear her say that, so I confirmed our mutual intentions.

She was standing next to Mary, the Mother of Jesus. As I turned toward her to say hello, I noticed some in the group began to kneel. Then some began to bow, and then finally all of them were kneeling or bowing, or they were putting their faces to the ground. Since they were all facing me, I didn't see Jesus walk up behind me. When I saw them do that, I immediately turned around to see Him, and when I realized He had come, I lay with my face on the ground in worship, and we were all worshipping Him together.

He touched me on my left shoulder. I instantly felt His warm love, the kind of love that's both unconditional and without bounds. As I stood to face Him, I wanted to embrace Him, but because of respect for Him and who He was, I was somewhat reluctant. I guess He instantly knew that, so He wrapped his arms around me. I can't begin to tell you how amazing it was to have the King of Kings wrap His arms around me. It's like being engulfed in the glory of God. There are no words to adequately describe this.

I still can't get over the fact that Jesus, the King of Kings hugged me, and it wasn't a little pat on the back kind of hug. I could tell that His hug was genuine and that He's not a wimp.

As we embraced, He told me that it was good to see me again. I indicated that I was excited to be there and was so glad to see him, but that I had a thousand questions to ask Him. I wanted to sit down with Him, just the two of us, when it was convenient. He indicated that He would do that, but not this trip, as I would not be there that long.

As we talked about my assignment, I felt His concern for both those who were still on the earth that are already His and for those who were yet to accept Him as their Savior. It was obvious to me that He knew the status of mankind on the earth and how morals and judgments were continuing to get darker and darker. Therefore, it was His plan that He would step up my trips so what

He had planned with me could be accomplished more quickly than originally thought. This would allow encouragement to both current believers and those who eventually would also become His. I indicated that whatever He wanted, that I was ready and willing. Once again, He complemented me on doing a good job for Him. When He said that, I told Him I was both excited and honored to do that. Then He greeted everyone else, gave a special hug to Mary, His mother, turned around, and walked off. We were all mesmerized with His visit, and for the first few moments, no one spoke. Even if we wanted to, I was not sure anyone could.

After what seemed like a few moments of silence, Rachel, my daughter, spoke up. "Daddy," she said, "I'm so glad to see you again." As she said this, she gave me a wonderful hug, then put her hands around my neck and gave me a wonderful hello kiss. "Are my mother and my brother still doing well? I'm very anxious to meet them both. Please give them a big hug for me, and let them know I'm looking forward to the day when I can do that myself. Wow, Dad, it's really good to see you. I always look forward to you coming. I know that you can't stay very long this time, but I'm glad you're here now."

I was just about to talk a little bit more with her when I noticed Cyberin and the chariot coming, so I knew it was time for me to leave. As I began to climb into the chariot, I heard the voice of a wonderful friend call my name.

It was Pearl. "Don't forget me," she said. As she stepped toward me, we greeted with a warm and wonderful hug.

"I could never forget you," I said. "Have you been enjoying your new life here?"

"Oh, yes," she said. "It's much more than I ever imagined. The Father has thought of everything. One of these times when you come, I'll have to show you around. I'm sure you'll enjoy it." I said I'd like that.

As I climbed into the chariot, I thanked everyone for coming. We began to pull away, and I waved goodbye, Cyberin waved, and all of those who had come to see me waved goodbye. Then we were off, and in just a few moments I found myself back in the living room sitting in my easy chair reflecting on the trip that had just taken place. I looked at the clock, which now read 1:52 p.m. I had been gone for thirty minutes.

Journey Number 36

THE GLORY OF GOD

O n Friday April 3, 2019, at three p.m., I heard His voice. He said, "Now is the time."

I said, "In the name of Jesus, I call for the traveling angel to come and pick me up." Then my spirit body left my physical body, and out the front door I went. When I stepped outside, Cyberin was there. He had his usual ear-to-ear grin, and he waved hello to me. I returned his smile and a wave, and I proceeded to step up into the back of the chariot, which was just floating in thin air. Then, without any hesitation, we were off.

This time, the journey went rather quickly, and before too long, I could see the bright light of Heaven. Cyberin and I didn't land in one of the usual locations this time, but from a distance, I could see where we were heading. This was the center of all things, the throne area. I was already excited to be taking another trip, but when I realized where we were going, I became even more excited.

When he stopped the chariot in the throne's general area, I knew I was in for a special treat. I said thank you to Cyberin for the ride. By now we'd become close friends. Once again, he acknowledged me with a smile and a wave, and off he went.

Now, standing there, the very first thing I noticed was the glory of God. It was much heavier here than in other places that I'd been. In other places, on a scale of one to ten, I would estimate that it was usually a five or a six. It was so much heavier here, that I was literally struggling to stay on my feet, and I would say it was an eight or nine. Using that same scale, if it was a ten, you would not be able to stand, so this was very close.

Now, without anyone around me to greet me, I found myself looking at this massive beautiful structure that words simply can't adequately describe, but I knew that inside sat the Creator of all things. I wasn't sure if I was allowed to venture inside, but I decided to give it a try. Before I did, I decided to look around a bit outside.

I couldn't get over the enormity of the structure. It was so large that I was unable to see from one end to the other. Next, I noticed the material used for the structure. I could tell that it was not marble, although it resembled it. But I could tell it was unlike anything I'd ever seen before. It's Heavenly for sure, and I have the sense that the material did not come from the earth, although as I said, it has the appearance of that similar to marble, as it glistens in the light.

I started to walk around, and before too long I found myself standing in the very area where I'd previously witnessed Jesus standing while he spoke to those already here, both human and angelic. I remembered that as He was preaching to the crowd, He was still teaching while at the same time encouraging them. While I was extremely humbled to be standing there, I couldn't get over how strong the glory of God was. This was not to say that the Father's glory is not in all of Heaven, because it is. However, this presence was definitely different, for it was much stronger there. In fact, at times it was so strong that I felt my knees buckling, so I was continually looking for something to grab hold of so I didn't fall. I looked out and saw others continually worshipping Him, even though He was not physically here. I joined in, and it was an awesome experience. I can't tell just how long I was there, but I do know it was more than just a few brief moments.

Next, I decided to see if I could go inside the structure. I wasn't sure if I was allowed to go in but thought that I'd like to try, and I began to look for a door. When I looked in the front, I noticed a huge single door that was closed, so I decided to walk up to see if it would open. As I approached it, still uncertain whether I would be allowed inside, to my amazement, it opened for me all on its own. That gave me the confidence that it was all right for me to enter.

Now I was walking through this massive door, and as I stepped inside, I was listening for sounds, music, voices, etc. I didn't hear anything. It was silent. I realized that I was standing in an entrance hall that must have led to a larger hall or rooms. I noticed that this entrance hall had several doors that could also lead to other places, so I decide to just pick one and go in and see what was going on. I wasn't sure which one to pick. They all looked inviting. I figured the center one was usually the most important, so I picked that one.

I opened the door to go in and was blinded by this enormous bright light. It was so bright that I couldn't look at it. In addition, my knees keep buckling, and I was fighting to stay upright. However, without looking at the bright light, and after a few moments, I was able to make out a few things. For the very first time in all of the trips to Heaven, I saw very ancient men who all had long gray or white hair and beards. They were all sitting around in a circle. Each of them had a crown in their hands, and they were continually bowing down in worship and presenting these crowns. I realized I was standing in the throne room of God. It was no wonder I couldn't stand.

I was there for what seemed like only a brief moment. I wasn't sure how I got out of there. I did feel that had I been there much longer, I would have been consumed by this bright light.

It was then time for me to leave, and I soon found myself back in the living room, sitting in my easy chair, convinced that I was not taken there to get instructions, but just to witness what I saw, for not only was it very real but I was also convinced that one of the reasons the Father sent His Son was because He, the Father, was so mighty that just standing in His presence would literally consume each and every one of us.

I look at the clock. It was 3:33 p.m. I'd been gone thirty-three minutes.

Journey Number 37

THE ANGELIC COURT

O n Friday, May 3, 2019, I was sitting in the living room when I heard His voice say, "It's time, come up here." I remembered to look at the clock. It read 2:02 p.m. I called for the traveling angel to come and pick me up, and out the front door I went. I wasn't surprised to see Cyberin sitting in the chariot with a smile on his face. I climbed in. This was quite a fast trip, for before I realized it, we were already there.

Waiting for us as we landed in Heaven was Abraham. I climbed out of the chariot and thanked Cyberin for the ride. Abraham and I greeted each other with a hug.

He said that it was good to see me again and that he was excited to be able to take me on this journey. "However," he said, "we are not going to walk there, for it is quite a distance. Flying will be our mode of transportation."

It didn't seem to take too long, even though we went quite a distance. We landed outside of a building that I hadn't been to before. Abraham informed me that it was a courtroom, but not for humans. It was an angelic court, which amazed me. This really peaked my interest. As we entered, I wondered if any other human had ever been inside or if I would be the first. Abraham must have known my thoughts, because he indicated that he'd been here a couple of times before.

We went inside, and I can't recall whether Abraham and I stood the entire time or eventually sat down. But there it was. It appeared to be just like a regular courtroom, just like those that are on the earth. However, it was all angelic, 100 percent.

There appeared to be an angel in charge, who was sitting on the bench, just like a judge would do. Another angel looked like he was taking notes with something. I watched as the first angel stood before the angel in charge. Both spoke in a language I didn't understand. With a smile on his face, the angel in charge seemed to be congratulating the other angel for a job well done. Then Abraham told me that this angel was given a promotion for his excellent work.

After the first angel was done, a second angel stood before the angel in charge. Even though I couldn't understand the words that were being spoken, it appeared as though charges were read for his not completing the task assigned to him. He didn't appear happy with what was read, and Abraham explained what was happening and that he was demoted in his rank for leaving his post. Abraham understand what was being said by the other angels.

I was amazed to see what was taking place before me. As we left the building, I had many questions. "You mean to tell me that there's an angelic court here in Heaven where angels are promoted or demoted for completing or not completing their assignments?"

"Yes," he said. "You have to remember that, just like humans, they also have a free will, and because of the number of angels the Father created, there are many of these courts here." Needless to say, I was stunned.

We flew back to where we had met earlier, and Abraham and I said goodbye. Then I heard someone behind me call my name. As I turned around to see who it was, I noticed a familiar face, along with a second person, I didn't immediately recognize. The person I did recognize was Paula. She had been my wife's best friend and had taken the journey to Heaven some twelve years earlier. When

I saw her last on the earth, she was in her late sixties and had blond hair. Now she appeared to be in her early thirties and had dark brown hair. She had a glow about her that no one could miss. With her was someone that I knew on the earth, but now, as she was standing there in front of me, I didn't recognize her.

Paula said, "You remember Paul's mom, my mother-in-law."

For a second, I just stood there looking at her. When I saw her last on the earth, she was a frail elderly woman. Standing there next to Paula, it looked to me like they were sisters. She had shoulder-length dark hair and was stunning. I could not get over how well she looked.

As we hugged, she told me it was good to see me again. She then told me how she remembered having dinner with her at her house in the church camp. She said, "We had steak and fried chicken with home grown vegetables and home grown corn on the cob."

I was amazed that she was able to remember that, for not only was it a long time ago, but she was remembering things that had happened while she was on the earth, even though she was now in Heaven.

"When you see my son Paul, if you're allowed to give him a message from me, please tell him I said hello, that I love him, that I'm continuing to pray for him, and that I look forward to seeing him here soon."

I told her that I felt that the Father would allow me to do that. Just then Cyberin and the chariot arrived, so I knew it was time for me to leave. We all hugged again once more, and I climbed into the chariot. Then we were off, and in just a few moments, I was back in my body, sitting in the living room easy chair. It was now 2:33 p.m. I'd been gone slightly over twenty minutes.

Journey Number 38

JESUS, ENOCH AND THE PROPHETS

Early in the morning on Friday, May 24, 2019, I heard the voice of the Lord say, "Come up here. I want to talk with you."

Before I knew it, I was there. Standing in front of Jesus, I started to go down to my knees. He caught me and pulled me upright.

"I'm glad to see you again," He said. "Before I introduce you to some of My friends, I want to take you on a short trip back in time."

It was as though I was looking at a large picture screen in front of us, as Jesus began to take us all the way back to when the earth was created, when He walked with Adam and Eve back in the Garden. From there, He took me to the time of Enoch, then Moses, and then Abraham. I was able to see them all in this overview of time.

"I was with them all as we walked together," He said. "These were all men of faith, and because of their faithfulness, I found them all to be men of righteousness."

As I watched, He brought us through the time of the prophets, Elijah, Elisha, and Ezekiel, followed by Daniel, and finally, Kings David and Solomon. We concluded with the lives of some of his disciples, John and Peter, followed finally by the conversion and ministry of Paul. There was so much material to consume from these various scenes that my head began to spin. He could see that I was having a difficult time with all of this material, so He said, "We'll pick it up at another time." Then He sent me back home.

The next day, Saturday, May 25, at 1:33 p.m., I wanted to go back again. It was still cool outside, so the doors to the house were still open. Sitting in my easy chair in the living room, I called for the chariot and driver. As I looked out the security screen door, I saw the chariot arrive, driven by Cyberin. To my amazement, Cyberin looked toward the door, and with his usual smile, he waved to me as though he was able to look through the security screen door and see me still sitting in my easy chair. While my physical body stayed in the chair, my spirit body went out to the chariot. I climb into the chariot, and we greeted each other again. However, I was speaking with Cyberin telepathically and not audibly. As we said our mutual hellos, we are off.

The trip to Heaven was not an extremely fast one, nor was it a slow one, and I once again was enjoying the wonderful beauty of the stars and planets, etc. The many colors of space were just breathtaking, and I doubted I'd ever get tired of such an amazing site.

Before I knew it, we were there. Heaven was such a wonderful and beautiful place, and I was enjoying the scenery as we came into a familiar place where I'd landed before. I wondered who, if anyone, would be there to greet me when I arrived.

As we approached our landing spot, I noticed someone standing there, and as we get closer, I realize that it was the Master Himself. Now I got very excited, almost breathless, and I saw Him, just standing there, waiting for Cyberin and me.

We landed, but before I could get out of the chariot, Cyberin stood up and bowed to Him. He said, "Hello, Master."

I started to stand in the chariot but didn't know whether I should bow or drop to my knees in the chariot or climb out of the chariot first and then drop to the floor. Without thinking about it, I climbed out of the chariot and planted my face on the floor in front of Him without saying a word.

Jesus gently pulled me to my feet. He said, "It's good to see you again. I've brought you here on this journey so you could visit with some of My friends, and for you to meet some of those that you have read about in My Word.

I heard someone approaching, and he said, "Hello Master." I didn't recognize Him, but he was the very first person I'd seen who looked to be very old. He had a full gray and white beard and all white hair. In all of the previous trips I'd taken, I'd never had the privilege of meeting anyone that looked to be very old, and I was somewhat taken aback.

Jesus asked me if I knew who it was, and I answer no. He introduced me to Enoch of the Old Testament, and I was just blown away.

I remember from reading about Enoch that he lived for three hundred and sixty-five years on the earth, but he never died, for God took him. I remembered reading that during his time on the earth, he had taken a total of eight trips to Heaven, and on the seventh trip, God told him he was going to be allowed to go back to the earth one last time, for a period of thirty days, and then, when he came up to Heaven for the eighth time, that would be his final trip; he would not be going back. I was amazed just to be standing and speaking with him.

My curiosity then got the best of me, so I wanted to ask him questions about his trips, what he saw, what he experienced, and what he'd been doing since he came the last time.

His response was quite simple. "Read his books."

I told him I remember it being referred to in Jude and that I not only had a copy of his books, but that I had already read them. However, to me it was quite confusing and way over my head. When I told him that, I expected him to say something comforting, but he said nothing. So I commented on the possibility of him showing me some of what he had learned while I was here.

He said, "Reread what I wrote. It will then become clearer."

I thanked him for his advice.

Just then, two other men approached. The first looked much like Enoch, in that he looked quite old. He also had a full beard that matched his hair, which was completely white. The second person who was with him looked like most of the people I'd seen there in that he also looked like he was possibly thirty, or somewhere around that age. He also had a fairly full beard, but both his beard and hair were dark brown or light black. Again, I didn't know who either one of these two men was. Jesus knew that, so He introduced me to both Elijah and Elisha.

Here I was, standing with Jesus, the King of Kings; Enoch; Elijah and his proteche, Elisha. I have to admit that I not only felt privileged but very humbled at the idea that I was standing in greatness to the max.

Then it hit me, and I turned to Elijah and asked him if he remembered being with Jesus while he changed on the Mount of Transfiguration? He just smiled and nodded. Then I asked both him and Enoch whether they would be the two witnesses of Revelation, chapter eleven. He smiled and nodded. It appeared that he was somewhat surprised that I would know that, but I couldn't help thinking that here I was standing alongside of men that had been on the earth more than three thousand years ago, and yet they were fully aware of their role in an event that not only hadn't happened yet, but could take several years from now before it would. Yet, to my amazement, they were fully aware of it and their role in it.

Then it was time once again for me to leave, as I noticed Cyberin and the chariot approaching. I didn't want to leave, but I knew it was time. I said my goodbyes to everyone and thanked Jesus for such a wonderful experience. He confirmed to me that these would become quite familiar with me as in future journeys they would meet with me to show me what they had been assigned. I thanked Him for that and bowed to Him. Then, into the chariot I climbed, and Cyberin and I waved our goodbyes.

My mind was so full of all that had just taken place that I didn't recall much of the return trip. I do recall sitting in my easy chair once again, thinking, "What just happened?" It was 2:22 p.m., and I realize I'd journeyed just under one hour.

Journey Number 39

TEA WITH RACHEL

M y next journey was on Friday, June 7, 2019. I can't tell just
how long I was gone because I didn't look at the clock
either before I left or when I returned.

It all started as I was once again sitting in my easy chair in the
living room. Earlier that day, I had decided it would be a good day
to take a trip, so as I sat there, I spoke those familiar words. "In the
name of Jesus, I call for the traveling angel to come and pick me up."

In a flash, my spirit body left my physical body, and I was out the
front door. There he was, Cyberin, my chariot driver, and his chariot
was just hovering in the front yard waiting for me.

We said hello to each other, I climbed into the chariot, and before
I knew it, we were off. Then I went back to my questioning about
how he operated the ship with just his thoughts, but all I could get
was, "I don't know, it just does."

I was very impressed. I looked for a steering wheel, steering laterals, dash controls, but nothing was there. "So then how does the
chariot know where to go just by your thoughts?" I said.

Once again, Cyberin simply smiled and said, "That's a question
you'll have to ask the Master the next time that you see Him."

I told him this would be one of a thousand questions I had. So
all I could do was sit back and enjoy the scenery, while at the same
time wondering who or what I'd see on this journey.

Once again, the scenery of space was just so spectacular. The clusters of stars with their vibrant colors, was totally out of this world. Looking at the stars with their vibrant reds, different shades of blue, different shades of green, golds, white, and purple, was amazing. When mixed, the colors made even new colors that I'd never seen before, but all were just breathtaking to look at. I felt so blessed to be able to do so. I'll never tire of seeing this.

Before I realized it, we were there. As Cyberin guided the chariot in, I noticed my daughter, Rachael, waiting for me. I was so excited to see her again.

As we came in and hover so I could stand up and exit the chariot, Rachel had the biggest grin on her face. I thanked Cyberin for the ride, and with a smile on his face and a wave, he was off. Now I was standing there all alone with my daughter.

Rachel and I hugged one another. I kissed her on the cheek, and as she continued to hold onto me, gave me a kiss on my right cheek, and said, "HI, Daddy. It's really good to see you again. I've waited for some time for this very moment."

I asked her if she knew if anyone else was coming, and she answered no. "Just me, Dad. I get to have you all to myself this time." She put her left arm in my right arm as we began to walk. I had no idea where she was taking me or if we were just going for a casual walk in Heavens Park.

"How is my mother doing?" she said. "Is she well? And how about my brother? Has he found someone special? I get so excited just thinking about you all and that time when we will all be here together."

As we continued to walk, we saw other saints near us who waved and said hello. Some of them called Rachel by her name, and she acknowledged them by their names. Then to my amazement, some said hello and called me by my name. I wondered how they knew my name.

To my pleasant surprise, Rachel knew where we were going. Soon we were standing in front of her house. It was good to see it again.

"I think we should have some heavenly tea while you're here, Dad. Would you like some of that?"

"Do you mean hot tea? I asked. "Yes, but we can have it anyway you'd want. You just need to think of how you would like it, and by the time that we go into the kitchen, it will be there, pot, cups, and all. And if you want anything to go in it, you just have to mention it, and it will also be there."

In all of my previous trips, I didn't remember drinking anything while in Heaven, so this would be a first for me. I thought, "How is this possible?" I was in my spirit body, and without any flesh, so how was this possible? Then I had to remind myself that He is the Alpha and Omega, the Beginning and the End. Anything is possible with Him. Not only that, but I was in His home here in Heaven. All things were possible here. I answered yes.

Just think, I was not only journeying back and forth from earth to Heaven, but if that wasn't enough, I was sitting with my daughter, who, by the way, was very much alive, and we were in her heavenly home sipping heavenly tea that just appeared when you wanted it and then disappears when you're through. "Praise the Lord!" I said. "I must confess, that this place is amazing, and I want to stay."

The tea had a familiar flavor to it, yet there was definitely something different about it. Without a doubt, it had the best taste for tea, and I really enjoyed just sitting in the kitchen with Rachel talking and having tea with her. Because I seemed to have so many questions, we mostly talked about what it was like living in Heaven. I asked her if she was ever bored here.

"Absolutely not," she said. She told me that there was always something for her to do.

We finished our tea and went into the living room. As we did, I turned around to see if the tea pot and cups we had just used were still there. To my amazement, they were all gone. They had just vanished. Nothing was left on the table.

Rachel must have known what I did, and how utterly amazed I was, so she said to me, "That's okay, Dad. You will get used to that happening here. It's really not a big deal. It's just the way it is here."

I reminded myself that this was all she'd ever known. Why would she be surprised. It's only me that was surprised. Just me!

I had a feeling that it was getting fairly close to the time when I would have to leave, so we walked out the front door. Two of her neighbors were out, so Rachael called to them to come over so that they could meet me. They were Hank and Doris. They had been husband and wife while on the earth. Rachel indicated that they had been married for sixty years before coming to Heaven. Although they were neighbors, they didn't live in the same house here. Doris lived right next door to Rachel, and Hank lived on the other side of Doris. I couldn't believe they'd been married that long. They both appeared to be in their early thirties.

From a distance, I could see Cyberin and the chariot coming to pick me up. As he brought the chariot close to the ground so I could get in, Rachel and I hugged and kissed each other goodbye. I climbed into the chariot, and Rachel told me she couldn't wait until I would be there permanently with her mom and brother. I told her it was so good to have seen her on this trip and thanked her for the time together and the tea, which I really enjoyed. Then we waved goodbye, and Cyberin and I were off.

I enjoyed the journey back to earth but must confess that my mind was full of reliving the time with Rachel. Then, before I realized it, we were back. I found myself once again in my physical body, sitting in the easy chair in the living room, not knowing just how long I'd been gone. All I can say is that I was ready to go again.

Journey Number 40

Journey with Elijah

On Thursday, June 20, 2019, at 9:07 in the morning, the house was quiet, so I thought it would be a good time for a trip. As I sat in my favorite easy chair, I spoke those all familiar words, and in an instant, I was once again sitting with my friend Cyberin in the chariot, and we headed toward Heaven.

Within what seemed like just a few seconds, we were about to land in Heaven in a place I'd landed before a couple of times, so it was somewhat familiar to me. There was no one there to meet me, but I stepped out of the chariot anyhow and thanked Cyberin for the journey. Once again, he just smiled, waved goodbye, and off he and the chariot went.

For a few brief moments I just stood there admiring the scenery of Heaven. It was such a beautiful place, always with its clear blue sky, luscious green grass everywhere I looked, its beautiful, perfectly shaped trees that were all surrounded by wonderful mountains in the distant background. Standing there and enjoying such a wonderful picture as this, not only did I not hear his footsteps as he approached, but I also do not know just how long I had been standing there just taking it all in.

Then he spoke. It was Elijah. Not just any Elijah, but the Elijah from the Old Testament, whom I had met just a couple of trips ago. He said hello to me, and I saw that he still had not changed. I am not sure why I thought that he might, but now he had the same very seasoned look about him that I saw when we first met some time ago in a previous trip. Also, I noticed that his voice was very deep and strong. I could tell just from listening to him speak that this was the voice of a leader.

"I've come to show you around a bit," he said.

Before I knew it, we were flying out of the city, across an open or country area, to another small city or rural area. This area was away from the main city area. It didn't seem like it was the outer portion of the main city, because there was some unoccupied country between the two cities. We landed in front of a beautiful mansion, which I could tell was quite large and appeared to have several floors. It was huge, and I commented to myself that it was without a doubt the largest home I'd seen so far.

"The Father built this for me," he said. "And I wanted you to see it. Isn't it beautiful?"

I was taken aback by its beauty and enormous size, especially when I remembered that when Elijah was on the earth, he didn't appear to have much of anything material to speak of. Obviously, he didn't need all of this, so I asked him why such a big place. His response was that the Father just wanted him to have it for all of the work he had done for Him, not only on the earth but continuing to this day. His workload for the Father still continued. He also commented that he was already aware of work he still had to do. I was just blown away. Needless to say, we stood there for some time, just looking at this marvelous workmanship as he explained certain things. I guess that, due to our lack of time, he never invited me inside. Obviously, he had other plans in mind.

I was curious as to how long he had been living in that house. He said it had been completed before he'd arrived, and he'd been using it ever since his initial arrival. The thought then occurred to me that he had lived around 500 to 600 BC, which would have been over twenty-five hundred years ago, and yet it looked like it had just been completed. I told him that it was just amazing!

Elijah then threw me another curveball. "What's it like on the earth now?" he asked. I asked him what he meant by that. "Well, are the living conditions the same today as they were when I was on the earth?"

"Absolutely not," I said. "Everything is different from when you were on the earth." I began to talk to him about some of the more modern changes, like automobiles, airplanes, trains, and motorcycles. I explained that houses today had indoor plumbing, refrigerators, and even heat and air conditioning. I told him about bathrooms, showers, beds for sleeping, and color television, all powered by the sun. When I finished telling him about each one, he just looked puzzled. I had to remind myself that he had come from a place and time that had none of these features. And yet, now, when he got hungry, he could just think of what he would like, and it just appears. Also, there was no waste there. When traveling, he could just think about wanting to go to a place, and he's instantly there. What a contrast between where he was, the timeframe that I currently live in, and his life here in Heaven for all of these years.

Then Elijah threw me a giant curveball, as he mentioned that he would like to go to my house where I lived on the earth and see it for himself.

"Are you able to do that?" I asked. He said he could, and as I turned around, there came Cyberin and the chariot.

Seeing this, I had so many questions. "How is it that you are able to do this? Is the chariot strong enough to carry the two of us? What about the added weight, and when we go, do we go the same way as I've been coming and going. Are you sure that the combined weight of you and me and Elijah make the chariot go slower?" Needless to say, we both climbed into the chariot. I was assured that everything would be just fine. And with that, we were off, headed back to the earth. I just couldn't get over it—Cyberin, Elijah, and me. Wow!

As we were steaming through space, Elijah commented that it had been a while since he had been out here, and he, like myself, just marveled at the beauty of space, with its breathtaking array of colors and clusters of planets and stars.

Before long, we were hovering in the chariot in the front yard of the house. As we stepped out, I was wondering how long we would be there, but I was assured that Cyberin was not leaving.

Elijah was just standing and looking at the front of the house. "So this is where you now live," he said. "With the mission that you are on for the Father, I would have thought that you'd have a much bigger house, but that will probably come, like mine did, when you come to the Fathers to stay."

I told him I'd already been allowed to see my future home but was not yet allowed to go inside. Then he surprised me and said, "That's probably because the Father has some very special things inside for you to enjoy, but they are reserved until you arrive there to stay."

So now we walked to the front door of the house, which opened on its own. I was blown away by that, and I thought that Elijah must have an unbelievable amount of power over all of the elements. Then I remembered that while he was on the earth, he called fire down from Heaven.

As we stepped inside, I showed him the living room, where my physical body was still sitting in the easy chair. I told him I'd been sitting like when I had taken many previous trips. He was curious to know if it had any significant purpose other than where I sat many times. I told him that to me it had, as I used it on a daily basis to visit with the Father and His Son, so it had special significance to me.

Next we went into the kitchen, where I introduced him to the range, oven, and microwave. I tried to explain to him how they all worked. I turned on the kitchen light, and he wanted to know how I was able to capture light, knowing how it is never dark in Heaven.

Running water was next, and he kept looking for the brook from which it flowed. I just laughed and told him it came from the center of the earth. However, the two things that astonished him the most were the cool air that kept coming out of the walls and the coolness of the refrigerator and coldness of the freezer. He was overcome with joy. I think he began to think about how things were when he lived on the earth and how much things have changed. Then he told me that he really liked living in Heaven and that it was unbelievably better.

Before we left, I wanted to show him how we traveled on the earth, so I wanted to take him out to the garage so he could see. He didn't look very impressed, knowing that where he currently lived, when he wanted to go somewhere, he just thought it, and he was there. I agreed with him and told him that I liked his way also.

He asked me about sleeping, so I took him down the hall to the master bedroom and showed him the bed. To my amazement, he went over and pushed down on it to see how soft it was. I must confess that when he did that, I wondered if he was going to lay down and try it out for himself, but he didn't.

He told me we needed to go, but before we did, I wanted him to see a bathroom. As he looked inside, he saw himself in the mirror and admired at how well he looked. I just laughed. Then I showed him a toilet, and he asked what that was for. I had to explain to him that in human form, we produce waste, both liquid, and solid. He wanted to know why, then he remembered his past. I reminded him that was the way that the Farther created us but that he should ask Him for more details. Then he reminded me that all heavenly bodies do not produce waste. I really surprised him when I flushed the toilet. He watched the water flow.

Now it was time to leave, and I was not sure if I was to travel back with him, but as we walked out of the house, he indicated that this was the purpose of this trip, and as such it was not necessary for me to return with him. Then I watched him climb back into the chariot. "Until we meet again," he said, and both he and Cyberin waved goodbye and were off.

This entire episode took a little under an hour; however, I went and sat in my easy chair to reflect on these things and am not sure just how long I sat there, for I must confess that by now, I just felt numb.

Journey Number 41

FISHING IN HEAVEN

O n Friday, July 5, 2019, at 9:07 a.m., the Father said to me, "Now is a good time. Come up here."

So, in a nanosecond my spirit body was out the door and into the chariot with Cyberin, and we sped toward Heaven, the Father's home.

When we landed and I'd climbed out of the chariot, once again Cyberin smiled and waved goodbye. Now I stood there alone, and before long I caught Him approaching. It was the Master, Jesus, and as he approached, once again I fell to my knees. Then in complete worship and submission, I lowered my face to the floor.

I was not sure how long that I stayed in this position, but eventually He helped me to my feet. Now facing Him, I could look right into His eyes, from which flowed the most wonderful love I could ever have imagined. Even though He was the King of Kings, I felt so warm and comfortable in His presence.

Then He spoke. "It's so good to see you again, Sam. Are you enjoying coming and going on these journeys? I can imagine that you must be having difficulty being in one world and then stepping into another, then having to travel back. I can tell from looking at you that there are times when you arrive back on the earth and yet a part of you is still here, isn't that true?" I had to confess that He was right, for there had been times when I know I was not always here.

Now I was walking with Jesus, and He has placed His left arm on my right as we walked. I didn't seem to care where, because I was just enjoying walking with Him. Also, I had all of the confidence in Him. Wherever we were going, he knew.

I was thoroughly enjoying walking with the Lord, so I was not paying attention to where He had us headed. However, He knew, and as we began to get closer, I figured out that He was taking us to the center of it all, to the throne room for a conversation with the Father. When I realized that was where we were going, my heart began to beat more rapidly.

As we stood outside of the building that houses the throne room, Jesus stopped and said we didn't have to go any farther. I can tell you that all of Heaven is filled with the glory of God. It was very tangible, but when I was close to the throne room, it was much stronger. For me, even though I was standing there with Jesus, the glory of God was so strong that it feels as though I could cut it with a knife. It was that strong. So now, for a brief moment, we just stood there, and then Jesus began to speak with His Father. As He spoke, it was as though His Father was standing right there beside us, for I could feel the glory of His presence descended heavenly on us. Once again I felt my knees buckling. I was glad Jesus still had a hold of my right arm, for He helped hold me up.

After acknowledging me, the Father began to speak to the two of us, first speaking to His Son, then with me. Much of what was discussed was about my coming and going. Then there were instructions for me that I am not allowed to put into writing, as they were of a personal nature.

When the Farther was finished talking with us, Jesus surprised me, for he said, "Let's go fishing."

I had no idea what fishing was like in Heaven, so at first I didn't respond. Obviously, He knew what He meant, and He knew I had no idea just what He meant. I told Him that I'd love to, but that I didn't know what that meant here in Heaven.

"Come on, let's go," His said, and before I realized it, we were both flying.

In what seemed like just a few seconds, we were landing beside a very large body of water. There was no one else around, and I didn't see any fishing nets or modern fishing equipment. Jesus could see the confused look on my face but just looked back at me and smiled. Then He said, "Let's go," and He started to walk into the water.

"Okay," I said. I started to walk into the water with Him, and soon we were up to our knees. Before long we were waste deep, then chest deep, and when the water was up to my neck, I turned to Him and saw Him going all the way under. I stopped to see when He would come up for air, but He didn't. I continued, and before long, there I was, fully submersed.

To my surprise, we were both now fully underwater, walking around just like it was the most natural of things to do. The water was crystal clear with a hint of blue, which I think came from the reflection of the blue sky. Then I heard Him speak to me, not audibly, but telepathically. We continued to converse as though nothing was different. I could not get over how naturally it felt, and the two of us continued to walk deeper and deeper. I must confess that this was a different experience, but I was so comforted, knowing Jesus was there walking with me all of the time.

The colors of plant life under the water are so amazing. I'd never seen these before. The fish under the water were also so brilliant in their colors. It was such a wonderful sight to behold, and I was constantly reminded of how beautiful Heaven is.

The fish kept coming around us, as though they were inspecting us. They were of all kinds, large and small. I didn't think they were as interested in me as they were Jesus, and I kind of got the feeling that they, in their own way, were bowing and praising Him, as though they knew Him. I continued to see them come up close for Him to touch them. This seemed to meet with their approval, and as He did, I could see a large smile on His face. It appeared that He was really enjoying Himself. Some of the fish also came up to me and let me touch them, but nothing like they were doing with Him.

Pretty soon we were done, and we walked out of the water back to dry land.

"I've taken you on a new experience here today," He said, "so that your mind would be expanded into something new, for you will experience a variety of different things here that you have not as yet experienced, so that you will be able to write about them. What you will experience will greatly encourage those that are still on the earth. Thank you once again for doing this for me."

With that He said goodbye, and it was time for me to return. Cyberin came to pick me up. In an instant, I was sitting in my easy chair in my physical body, reflecting on what had just happened. It was now 10:22 a.m. I had been gone over one hour.

Journey Number 42

THE RECORDS ROOM

O n the morning of Tuesday, July 16, 2019, I took another
journey. I started somewhere around nine thirty to nine forty-five. The time is not as important as the substance of what I am
about to write of this journey.

Once again, I was sitting in my easy chair in the living room
and thought that this would be a good time to take a trip. No one
had previously spoken with me and called for me to come; I just
elected to go. So, without hesitation I said, "In the name of Jesus,
I call for the traveling angel to come and pick me up."

Then, without me thinking about it, my spirit body left my
physical body, and out the front door my spirit body went. Cyberin
was in the chariot, just waiting for me. As I approached, he smiled
his usual big grin. I sat down, and we were off.

I was curious to learn just how long Cyberin had been doing
his job of operating the chariot. "Have you been doing this for
very long?"

He smiled again and just nodded his head. This led me to
wonder if, in the past, he had picked up other people, and I wondered if he continued to do that now. "Are there others?" I asked.
He continued to smile and nod. So that led me to several other
questions. "How long have you been around? Were you here when
the Father created the Heavens and the earth during the six days of
creation?" He looked at me and asked me just how I knew about

those things. I told him that I had read about it in Gods Word. Then he told me that he was around and remembered the great falling away of angels. "That was not a happy time in Heaven," he said.

Next I wanted to know more of things in the past that went on in Heaven, but our journey there was almost over, as we were about to land. When we came to a stop, we were fairly close to a very large building, and as I started to exit the chariot, I thanked Cyberin not only for the trip, but also for answering several of the questions that I had. He then pointed me to the large building and told me that in the building I would find the answers too many of the questions that I had.

I stood there for a brief moment and watched as Cyberin and the chariot took off and eventually went out of sight. Then I turned around and walked to the building. When I got to the door, it didn't open on its own for me, which I thought was kind of strange, so I grabbed a hold of the door handle and opened it.

Inside were rows and rows of shelves, up as high as I could see and down for as long as I could see. On the shelves were what looked like black books, all of the same size and color. I discovered that I was now standing in the records building, and I could not see the end of it. I was curious about this building. First, I can't tell you just how large this building was. It looked like it went on forever; it was that large. For as high as I could see, there were rows and rows of shelves, all lined with these black books. Then, looking down one row, I saw they lined both sides. I was curious about what these all were. I was then told by one of the angels that had come up to meet me that it was in this building that all of the records of all humanity were housed, as well as all of the records of all of the angelic beings ever since the beginning. Each one of the books contained the life of one person or angel, to include all of everyone's thoughts, everything that they had ever said, and everything that they had ever done.

I looked down the main hall, and there I could see one book sitting by itself. It was on its own pedestal. The pedestal seemed to be made out of a material that looked like marble, and the book was golden. It was opened, and it looked like sunlight was coming out of it. I thought that this book might be the Lamb's Book of life, and my curiosity got the better of me, so I thought I should go over and check it out, especially since it was open. I thought that if it was the Lamb's Book, it might be opened to my name.

I know that I know that I know that my name is written in the book.

As I was walking toward the book, one of the angels indicated to me that I was correct, that the book was the Lamb's Book of life and that in it were the names of all of the people who were declared righteous in God's sight because they had declared His Son (Jesus) as their Lord and Savior. Now I was standing in front of the book and looking at the name on the open page. I was not sure if it read Johnson, or Johansen, but I do know that it was not opened to my name. I wanted to turn the pages to my name but felt that this was a book I should not touch. So, I didn't.

Then I walked over to one of the shelves, where one of the angels was standing. He then took one of the books off the shelf and opened it. As I looked at the pages he had opened it to, all of a sudden a large screen came out of the page and presented a panoramic motion picture in front of us, from start to end, of the events that has been recorded on that particular page in the life of the individual whose name was on the front of the book. Since the angel was holding the book, which was now opened, I never did get to notice the individuals name on the book. As I watched scenes unfold, if I had a question, the angel that was holding the book would explain various things to me.

However, I did notice something else. Evidently this individual's name must have also been written in the Lamb's book of life, for as the event that had been recorded in the open page that I had been reviewing came to a conclusion, the angel holding the book turned to another page, and when the screen came out of the book for that page, the screen was blank. I asked the angel why the screen was blank, and he said that not only are all of the events in the life of a human recorded, that being everything that one had ever thought, had ever spoken or done, in addition, all of the events of all angels were also recorded in their own book as well. So here on the pages of someone's book where the pages are blank, an event occurred wherein the individual, either in thought or deed, committed a sin against the Father and had repented of that event, had asked for forgiveness, and because of the request by the individual, the sin that originally was in the book was remembered no more. That is why the page was whipped clean, for the event was forgotten. Wow, I could not believe just how easy that worked.

Then the angel almost knocked me to the floor when he told me that all of the angelic beings from the beginning up to now and all down through time each had their own book and would be judged on the Day of Judgment for what they had done, thought, or said. I had never thought of that. He told me that their books were stored somewhere other than where we were standing. He asked me if I would like to see them, so we headed to where they were stored.

We walked for quite a while and ended down several rows and halls inside the same building, but eventually we stopped where he thought we should be. I had asked him if he could take me way back in time to the very beginning, to an event that occurred involving an angel or angels.

When we got to where he wanted to go, he stopped and pulled out another book and opened it up. Just like the previous book, when it was opened, a screen appeared in front of us revealing the time when God spoke and the earth was created. Next, I watched as the first man (Adam) appeared, and then Eve was created. She was a very beautiful woman, one that one day I would like to meet on one of my trips, for I have many questions I would like to ask her.

As I continued to watch, and as time continued and man continued to populate all the earth, I saw that angels were sent to watch not just over the earth but over man's occupation of the earth as well, and I was told that a group of angels, who numbered two hundred strong, were assigned to various places all over the earth. Their job was to watch all of the events that were going on, and they were required to report those events back to Heaven as those events were taking place. These two hundred angels were called watchers.

As I continued to watch, the angel that was with me told me that less than one thousand years had passed since Adam was created and mankind had begun to walk on the earth. It was during the time of Jared, Enoch's father, who was the fifth generation from the time of Adam, that the population greatly multiplied on the earth, with an explosion of people being born everywhere. The angels who had been assigned to watch over the affairs of the on goings of mankind on the earth and report those findings back to Heaven, called watchers, then looked upon the daughters being born to men and saw how beautiful they were and lusted after them and said to one another, "Let us choose wives for ourselves from among the women on the earth." (I think Genesis 6 refers to this.) Then all of them together, including their leaders changed their appearance to look like masculine human gods, which were very attractive to the women, and they came down and took for themselves wives, each one choosing one for himself, and they defiled themselves, even taking some of the women from their husbands, and they had sex with these women. Then the women became pregnant, and their offspring, the union between mankind and angels became giants in the land. These giants were called Naphilim. As they grew, they became extremely disfigured, and mankind began to fear them because of their size and appearance. This is where mythology came about.

God caused the children of the watchers and the earthly women to fight against one another so that they might destroy each other.

Soon mankind began killing one another, along with anything that moved on the face of the earth, and when God saw this, He was very displeased.

When God created all of the angels, they were to live for all of eternity. In other words, they would never die. However, since these watcher angels, who still would never die even after committing such a sin against God continued to live, it was their human angelic offspring that eventually would die, but only that part which was human. The angelic spirit part would still continue to live on, and these became known as demons or evil spirits. They are the disembodied spirits of the offspring of humans and angels.

It was during this time that God found favor with one righteous man who was still living on the earth, whose name was Enoch. He lived for 355 years and then disappeared because God took him to be with him. God had Enoch go and speak to the watchers and told them of the deed that they had committed, so they together asked Enoch to prepare a petition for them that they might find forgiveness for their deeds. They asked that he take the petition before the Lord. Enoch did so, but the petition was not granted, and judgment was passed on these watchers. They were confined to the earth for all eternity and were not allowed to ever enter Heaven again. These angels that had sinned against God were all sent to a place where they were imprisoned, and required to stand and stay until the great Judgment Day.. (I think this is in referred to in 2 Peter 2:4.)

God saw how that the wickedness of mankind was great on the earth. So God decided He would destroy the whole earth with a flood, to cleanse it of its iniquities. He gave instructions to Noah, a righteous man, to build an ark, and when the ark was finished, it was filled with all kinds of animals and birds, and Noah and his family entered the ark. Then God shut the door, and for forty days and nights, rain fell from the sky, and waters from the depths of the earth were opened up. As a result, all of the earth was flooded, and all air-breathing creatures that were not in the ark died. This is the way that God purified the earth.

Then the angel holding the book closed it. He looked at me and saw that everything I had just been shown made my face as white like snow. He knew I had seen enough for now. So he helped me to walk back to the front of the building to where the door was, and when he saw Cyberin and the chariot arrive, he lead me out of the building and into the chariot. Then Cyberin and I were off, but we didn't speak to each other during the entire trip back to earth. I didn't recall exiting the chariot, but I must have, for the next thing that I recall was sitting in my easy chair, reconnected with my physical body in the living room. I have no idea how long I was gone this time. I must confess that I have been numb from this experience.

Journey Number 43

CYBERIN AND THE FALLEN WATCHERS

E arly on Thursday, August 2, 2019, I went on another trip to Heaven. Cyberin, picked me up, as usual. Earlier, I'd heard the Master's call, so off we went. However, the trip was not a direct journey from earth to Heaven. Instead, Cyberin took us to a place somewhere below the earth, a very dark place, and told me that this was the place where the watcher fallen angels were being held. There, they had been sent and were placed within a dungeon. Here they were to remain until the Judgment Day for their sin against the Father of leaving their Heavenly posts around the earth and uniting themselves with women of the earth. There appeared to be some kind of mist or cloud surrounding the area.

As the chariot stopped so I could get a fuller view, Cyberin began to explain to me what was going on here. Without looking up, one of the fallen angels called watchers asked if he could speak. Somehow he knew we were there and that we were on our way to Heaven. We spoke telepathically. He asked if I would go to the Father on their behalf and ask Him for forgiveness so that they could be freed once again from where they were being held, and once again be allowed to enter Heaven. I must confess that I was stunned by his request. Needless to say, I didn't respond that I would, nor did I say that I would not. We stayed there for just a brief moment more, and then were once again on our way to Heaven. By the time that we got there, I was still somewhat in shock, still thinking about what I had just seen and the request that had been made.

As we arrived in Heaven and Cyberin brought the chariot to our destination, there the Master, Jesus, was standing, just waiting for Cyberin and me to arrive. I had seen Jesus standing there before we stopped, so when we finally did stop and I exited the chariot, I fell to the floor in worship.

After telling me to rise, He began helping me to my feet, and as I looked at Him, He told me that it was good to see me again. I still couldn't get over looking into his eyes, which were full of love for me. He knew that we had just come from the place where the fallen watcher angels were, and He knew the request they had made, because He immediately began to talk with me about their request. I didn't bring it up to discuss; He did.

He said, "The Father has already made His decision regarding this matter, and has not changed His mind. He has placed them where they are, and they are to remain there until the Judgment Day, when He will judge them for their disobedience and deeds. Therefore, the mater remains closed until then."

I was somewhat relieved, for ever since the request was made, I had felt uncomfortable and I believe that Jesus already knew this, and this was the reason that He spoke about it right from the beginning. Therefore, once He said this, we didn't speak of it anymore.

There was other items the Lord and I talked about that related to additional trips I would be taking, along with some personal matters, none of which I will include in this book.

Eventually, we said our goodbyes, and Cyberin came to pick me up in the chariot. Soon I was back in my physical body, sitting in the easy chair and reflecting on this journey. I was gone all of twenty-two minutes this time.

Journey Number 44

HEAVENS ORCHESTRA AND
THE SOUND OF COLOR

O n Friday, August 16, 2019, my journey started at 8:55 in
the evening. I heard the Master say, "Come up here. I want
to see you and visit."

However, rather than calling for Cyberin and his chariot to
come and pick me up, in an instant, my spirit body left my physical
body there in the living room, and I was there in Heaven standing
before the Father's Son, Jesus.

Upon seeing Him, my immediate reaction was to plant my face
on the floor in worship. He then helped me to my feet, and we
greeted each other with a heavenly hug. He is such a blessing just
to be around, and I always want to just hang out with Him. Then
he surprised me when He asked what I would like to see or learn
about. This was quite unusual. I didn't believe that on any of my
previous trips I'd been asked about what I wanted to see or learn
about. Usually, all of the previous trips had a predetermined purpose to it, which was preplanned for me, and so to hear Jesus ask
me what I wanted to inquire about, see, or ask, found this very
interesting. I indicated to Him that I would like to see the heavenly
orchestra, because in all of my previous trips, no matter where I
went, whether it was inside or outside, music was always abundant,
and so I was curious as to where the orchestra was and just how it

was that I was able to hear it wherever I was, whether I was in the city, out in the out skirts, or even in the mountains. When I told Him that, He just looked at me and smiled. By His grin, I knew there was something to my request.

"Look around and see all of the colors. The music that you hear comes from all of these colors that you see," He said. He could see the puzzled look on my face, and He knew that I didn't understand. "First, as you will notice, here in my home there are a lot of different colors, much more than what is on the earth, and the colors that you are familiar with, they appear to be much more alive then what is on the earth. Each color here has a tone, and while these tones are praising the Father, they make the music that you hear. The Father, in His creativity, made the colors so each would have its individual tone or sound, and with His creativity, He has made the colors and their tones to harmonize together with all other colors, and it is their tones that make up the music that you hear. So, as you look at the grass, it is praising the Father in its tone. Then the trees also have their tone while at the same time they too are praising the Father. Even buildings, with each ones particular color, have their tone as they praise Him in worship. The structures in the city all harmonize together in worship, while the forests in the mountains do the same from where they are. The trees with their specific color that produce fruit have their own tone. So, as you can see that everything that is here has its own color or colors with their particular tones. Together, they make the orchestra that you want to see. If you take just a few moments to look around, you can see the orchestra; it's all around you. The Father has thought of everything. I must confess that when He told me that, I was just blown away with this information."

When He explained this to me, I had to look around at all of the wonderful things that are here in Heaven, and I must confess that it was with a different outlook that I now looked at all things.

Then I had to ask Him, "Well, then is there such a thing as a heavenly orchestra?"

"Absolutely," He said. "And I will take you to see them at a different time. This is enough for now."

I knew then that it was time for me to leave, but I had to ask Him one final question. "So, you mean to tell me that all buildings, and their individual materials, if they are different than other building materials, all have their own color and therefore tone?"

He said, "Yes, just as one color has many sub-colors to it, then these building materials each have a slightly different tone, if it has a slightly different material used in its construction, which then gives it its own blended tone. So if you looked at a street made of dirt, it would have a certain tone, while a street of yellow gold would produce a different tone, and yet the streets in the New City Jerusalem, made of the purest white gold produce a different tone."

I thanked Him for the explanations and the time that we had spent together, and before I knew it I was sitting back in my physical body in the easy chair. Even though I was only gone for fifteen minutes, I sat in the easy chair for quite a while, not able to move while at the same time contemplating the time that I had just spent with Jesus, and all that I had just seen, and heard.

Jesus, He is the Alpha and Omega, the beginning and the End, second person of the Trinity, Jehovah, Prince of Peace, and King of Kings. Praise His name!

Journey Number 45

AT HOME IN NEW JERUSALEM

O n Thursday, August 22, 2019, the journey started at five fifteen p.m. and lasted sixteen minutes. I decided that would
be a good time to take a trip, and so I spoke those all too familiar
words. "In the name of Jesus, I call for the traveling angel to come
and pick me up."

When I said that, my spirit body left my physical body, which
was still sitting in the easy chair in the living room, and out the
front door I went to an awaiting chariot and driver in the front yard.
Cyberin acknowledged me with his huge, angelic grin. When I got
into the chariot, he turned around to make sure that I was ready,
and off we went.

As usual, the ride to Heaven was, without a doubt, just breathtaking. We didn't head toward the sun but seemed to travel for a
short while in a direction that was ninety degrees to the right of the
sun. After a short while, Cyberin headed the chariot in the direction
toward a large cluster of various colored stars, and I must admit
that traveling toward them was very enjoyable to see, at first from
a distance, then much closer, and finally I was elated as we eventually were just surrounded by them. Their beauty just got to me,
and while I was not sure if you breathe when in your spirit body,
the wonder of what I was seeing literally took my breath away. I so
enjoyed being surrounded by the beauty of these clusters of multi
clusters of stars. At one point, Cyberin must have been able to read

my thoughts, as I wondered whether I could operate the chariot. His response was that I probably could; however, I didn't know the way we needed to go. He was right about that, and I thanked him for letting me know. I was glad he was here doing his job.

Heaven is without a doubt the brightest place in all of the cosmos. While you can't see it from different places in the cosmos, as you get closer to it, when you are able, it stirs something within you, and for me, it's no exception. Once it came into focus for me, I always seemed to become excited, and this was no exception. I wondered what was in store for me on this trip.

As Cyberin directed the chariot to the designated landing area, there waiting was a wonderful familiar face. It was Abraham. As I climbed out of the chariot and we greeted, he said, "Hi, Sam. It's great to see you again. I've been looking forward to this time that we have together. The Father has instructed me where He wants us to go so that you may learn a bit more."

As we started to walk away, I turned around and thanked Cyberin for the ride. He just smiled and waved his usual goodbye.

Now Abraham and I started walking, to where I didn't know, but I was comfortable with him being my guide on this trip. I knew that wherever we were going, I could trust Abraham, for he had not disappointed me in any of our previous encounters.

As we walked, we talked, and first he let me ask about what it had been like to be here in Heaven for such a long time. I told him that in earthly years he had been here for over four thousand years.

He said, "Wow, that seems like a long time." But being here, he had absolutely no concept of time, as it seemed like just yesterday that he arrived here. I was surprised to hear him say that and was blown away with his comments.

About that time, he told me where we were going, and it became obvious, as we were heading toward the New City Jerusalem. However, this time, when Cyberin and I had landed, we were close enough that I thought we might, and since we were that close, it didn't require Abraham and me to fly anywhere, as we had before, so we just walked to the entrance.

As we approached this huge city within Heaven, I could not help but marvel at its outside beauty and enormous size. I remember reading about it in Revelation that it was as tall as it was long and as wide as it was tall. I was told that it was a cube. Some say it's fourteen hundred square miles, while others say that it's fifteen hundred square miles. At the outside of the city, at the bottom or its foundation, were twelve different colors, all laid in layers, which I was told represented the twelve tribes of the Nation of Israel. The balance of the structure appeared to be made of the finest and purest clear white gold. Now don't get me wrong. The earth has its beauty, while Heaven also has a beauty that by far outshines earth. However, this city was by far the most beautiful structure I'd ever laid my eyes on. It was breathtaking, to say the least. There are no words to describe what the Father had created here. And that's just looking at it from the outside. To think that one day saints from all ages will be able to call this place home is simply unimaginable. It is no wonder that one would have to be in their new or glorified body to live there.

As I was standing there trying to take in all of the beauty of the outside of the structure, Abraham said, "Let's go inside." It was as though he was also curious. He knew that once inside, we would see places and things that he hadn't seen before either. So, we approached one of the gates, which was already opened, and we just walked in. There were no angels guarding the entrance to the city.

As we walked in, I could not get over how quiet it was. To me it felt like we had just stepped into hallowed ground. I thought of Noah and how he must have felt as he walked into the ark from one floor to the other when it was finished, just before the animals were brought into it. Clearly, he probably had the same feeling as I was having looking at this huge but empty surroundings.

I looked over at Abraham, and his eyes seemed to be opened as large as mine. It was obvious that we were on the ground floor. I looked toward the ceiling, but could not see where it ended. I asked Abraham if he could see the top. He said that he could not. However, he then informed me that he was told that this city had many levels to it.

"Do you know how many?" I asked.

"No," he said. "All I have been told is that it has many."

"Do you know who stays on one level or the other?"

His answer was that he was not informed about this matter.

As I looked around, it appeared that the entire city was made out of the finest white gold–looking substance. It looks to be so fine that it was almost clear, so clear that one could almost see through it. That is except for the streets. I was able to recognize them as solid gold. Each building was made out of this pure clear or white gold. It was magnificent to look at.

"Where do people live?" I asked. "Do you know? Can we go there?"

Abraham said it was on a different level. I asked him if we were allowed to go there. He said we were, so I wanted to know how it was that we could get from one level to another.

His answer was almost funny. "Come on. Let's go." He grabbed my hand and, in an instant, we were on another level. I was not sure just how we got there, for I do not remember flying. It was as if one instant we were on one level, and then in another instant we were on another.

"I'm not sure which level we're on," he said. "Let's look around and see what we can see." Based on his comment, I was pretty sure he hadn't been here before either.

"I wonder just how many levels there are here," I said.

His response just floored me. He said, "Many."

Then, within what seemed like a few short moments, we were on another level, then another. I was not sure how many levels we went to, but it was more than two or three. As we had traveled from one to another, I was told that we had not gone from level one to level two and then three but had skipped around a bit.

On one of the levels, Abraham said to me, "I'm not sure which level we're on now, but I do know we're supposed to stop here so you can see something that's especially for you, for the Father has made this for you and wants you to see what He has done. As we walked for just a little while, there before me was my home, just like the one I'd been taken to in Heaven. I could not believe my eyes. It was identical to it. Abraham's comment was that the Father knew me so well that He knew how much I'd enjoy living in it, so He had decided to remake it and place a duplicate of the one that was originally created for me, and so all the while I'd be living in this new city, this would also be my home. When he said that, you could have knocked me over with a feather. I was that floored, for there it was, my home.

As we departed the city, I noticed my daughter Rachel standing outside waiting for us. I thanked Abraham for the tour and asked him if he had ever met Rachel before. He said that he had, and at the same time, he said hello to her. The two of them hugged. It was interesting for me to see this and to see how the two of them interacted with each other. Rachel said to me that she had been told I was here, so she wanted to see me again. Once again, I thanked Abraham, and as he started to leave, Rachel and I hugged for quite a long time. I kissed her on her forehead, and she put her arms around my waist and kissed me on my right cheek.

"It's so good to see you again, Daddy," she said. "I have been wondering when you would be coming again so that I could see you. Have you had many trips since I saw you the last time?"

I had to confess that my comings and goings have been so many that I wasn't able to properly answer her question. She noticed the puzzled look on my face. "I understand, Dad," she said.

I told her that I had thoroughly enjoyed each journey, for they all seemed unique in their own special way, and I knew I was nearing the completion of the first of four books. When I told her that she was in several chapters of the book, she seemed quite surprised, yet pleased.

Cyberin and the chariot approached, so I knew my time there was just about up.

"Please tell my mother and brother that I said hello," she said. "And when you see my grandmother, please say hello to her for me, and let her know I'm looking forward to seeing her here soon and spending some special time with her, just the two of us. After all, even though we have never met, I have heard so much about her that I feel that I already know her, and I believe that we have a kindred spirit."

I assured her I would relay the message.

We hugged and kissed once more, and I climbed into the chariot. We waved goodbye to each other, and as we started to leave, Rachel blew me a kiss.

Then we were off. The journey back was just as wonderful and glorious as the trip there, which I enjoyed thoroughly, as eventually the earth came into view. I'm not sure if I've said this before, but looking at it yet from some distance, it is without a doubt the most colorful of all of the planets.

Before I knew it, the journey was over, and I was sitting back in my physical body in the easy chair of the living room. This was such a wonderful trip. It was now 5:31 p.m. All of this had taken place in just sixteen minutes, and I think I was ready to go again.

Journey Numbers 46 and 47

Two Times the Charm

O n Monday, September 23, 2019, I took two trips. The first
one started at 2:21 p.m. and lasted until 2:49 p.m., which
meant that I was gone for a total of twenty-eight minutes. The
second trip was an extension of the first one. I left the same day, at
2:52 p.m. and returned at 3:01 p.m. I was gone for just nine minutes.

Let me explain. A few days earlier, while I was in prayer, the
Lord spoke to me and told me that I would be traveling on Monday.
In addition, He told me that I would be seeing some familiar faces.
He also said I'd see someone I knew but hadn't seen in many years.

I was sitting in my easy chair in the living room and thinking
that now would be a good time to take a trip. I said, "In the name
of Jesus, I call for the traveling angel to come and pick me up."
Without thinking about it, as though it was quite natural or usual,
up out of the easy chair my spirit body went, leaving my physical
body, and out the front door I went to a waiting chariot and driver,
who was just waiting for me in the front yard.

Upon seeing me, Cyberin extended his usual big smile. As I sat
down, off we went. I must confess, it was good to see him again, so
I told him that. He just smiled and nodded at me, indicating that he
was glad to see me also. It wasn't until then that the realization hit
me that I was once again on my way, and my excitement grew as I
recalled the conversation that I had had with the Lord. I wondered,

who would I see that was familiar, and who was I going to meet that I haven't seen for quite a long time.

Before I knew it, the journey there was coming to an end. I commented to Cyberin that he really kicked in the afterburner this time. He said he was told to get me there quickly. There were those already waiting for us. I couldn't get over the different modes of travel there: 1) like lightning, 2) the speed of sound, and 3) the speed of thought.

When we came to where we were to stop, there were three people waiting—my earthly father, one of my brothers, named Bill, and my daughter Rachel, who had never made it to earth. I exited the chariot, and before I acknowledged anyone, I thanked Cyberin for the ride and said I would see him in a while for the trip back. Then I greeted my dad with a hug.

He said, "It's good to see you again, son." I could tell something was up, or he knew something I didn't know, for he had this grin on his face like I had seen on him at times while he was still alive and on the earth. It looked like he had been caught with his hand in the cookie jar. It was a grin that when you saw it, you knew that he was up to something or knew something. I would find out very quickly.

Next, I turned my attention to my brother Bill. As we hugged, he said, "It's really good to see you again, Sam. How have you been? How is Donna and Sammy, Mom and all of my other brothers and sisters? By the way, I've been meaning to tell you something. Thanks for praying for me. I'm so happy here. This is the happiest I've ever been. I love it here, and I know that you were praying for me, because you told me that you were. I know there were others too, but they're not here, and you are. So thank you, and do me a favor. Tell all those others thank you also. I'm here in part because of your prayers. I didn't realize it then, but I do now, and I really appreciate all of the prayers."

I was shocked. He was the first person I'd met there in Heaven that had said thank you for taking the time to pray for them. I was so encouraged by that, well I just can't explain it, for it is true that all down through eternity, we will meet some we've had just a little part in bringing there. I was so happy for him.

I've thought about those words to me and others and just how important our prayers really are. They will play a part in the lives of those who ultimately will be there for all eternity. Wow, what a privilege.

I could hardly wait to put my arms around my daughter Rachel and give her a wonderful fatherly hug and kiss.

"Hi, Daddy," she said, as she hugged me back and planted her kiss on my right cheek. I didn't think I'd wash my cheek for quite a while. It was so good to see her. Then she put her left arm in my right arm just held on to me for quite some time, while we all talked, caught up and laughed for the next few brief moments. They wanted to know what I had been doing, and I wanted to know about them.

As we were talking, another man approached whom I didn't recognize. My dad said, "You don't know who this man is, do you, son?"

I told him I did not. So Dad introduced me to Reverend Allen. As he extended his hand to me, he said, "I know you. When you were a little boy, I was the pastor of the Christian and Missionary Alliance Church in Rochester, New York. Your parents took your whole family to the church there, where I was pastoring, and my wife and I became close friends with your parents. So, when your mother was pregnant and about to give birth to your sister Sue, you and your brother Dave came and stayed with my family for a few days. I also knew your brother Bill. He was more of a challenge than you were."

My Dad spoke up and said that all through his life, Bill always was a challenge. The pastor said he was glad that we had both made it here. (It seemed like he didn't know my assignment.) "By the way," he said, "When you kids were growing up, we seemed to have had an abundance of tires going flat during the evening Sunday services in the parking lot. You guys don't remember anything about that, do you?" I just smiled and looked at Bill, who was also just smiling. We didn't say a word, but I was surprised that even though he had been here in Heaven for quite some time, here was an episode that he clearly remembered from the past. Also, they seemed very clear to him.

As the reverend turned to walk away, I could see Cyberin coming for me in the chariot, so I knew my time here was just about over. Dad and I were the first to hug. As we did, he said he wanted me to know that many there had been assigned to continue to pray for me during the term of my assignment. He just wanted me to know. Bill and I hugged next, and he reminded me of his earlier request. I assured him that I would let everyone know just how important our prayers really are, and that he was a prime example of it, and as a result, I would tell everyone that I could.

Finally, Rachel and I started toward the chariot together, holding onto each other. It was as though we didn't want to let each other go. But I knew that I must, so we kissed each other and hugged. As she kissed me, just like before, she asked me to say hello to her mother and brother for her and remind them that she was a bit anxious to see and spend time together with each one of them.

"I love you Dad" she said. "And please let them know for me that I love them also."

As I climbed into the chariot she said, "I know you have a job to do for the Father, but if you can, please hurry back soon."

We all waved goodbye, and Cyberin and I were off. It wasn't long before I found myself sitting back in my physical body in my easy chair in the living room.

I sat there for some time, still in shock from the journey just completed and trying to absorb all that I'd just experienced. The clock now read 3:49 p.m., so I knew I had been gone for twenty eight minutes.

Then I heard His voice speak to me for a second time. "Do you want to go again?" He said.

"Yes," I said.

I kind of expected the Lord to say, "Well, okay, how about tomorrow or the day after that?" But that was not His intention. He meant right now.

Then it happened in just an instant. I was back in Heaven. However, I had not been picked up by Cyberin in the chariot, nor had I traveled at the speed of light, but I'd journeyed within a microsecond at the third speed of Heaven, which is the speed of thought, for in that microsecond, there I was now once again standing in front of the same three people that I had originally been with just a few minutes before. There was my Dad, my brother Bill, and my daughter Rachel. They were all standing in the same place we had just met, and as I realized where I now was and who it was that was standing with me. I began to wonder just how they knew that I would be returning within just a few brief moments. Also, how did they know where I would be returning to, and when? So, I began to ask them.

Their responses were all the same. They said they just knew. The Spirit of the Father resided within them and revealed these things to them. Needless to say, when they explained it that way to me, it made a lot of sense.

All three of them were facing me kind of like not quite a semi-circle, so they didn't see Jesus as He was approaching from behind them. However, I did, and as I realized that it was He who was coming, I began to drop to my knees. As I did, the others saw what I was doing and instantly knew, and they began to bow before the King. As Jesus approached, I fell to the floor, but I heard my Dad and Bill acknowledge Him to each other as King Jesus. Rachel on the other hand said, "Hello, Master."

Since my face was planted on the floor, I heard Jesus speak as He told us to rise. I didn't know if my Dad and my brother Bill were bowing or kneeling, but as I began to stand, I heard my brother Bill speak first.

He said, "It's really good to see you again, King Jesus."

My dad, on the other hand, was speechless. I think he was overwhelmed by the presence of the Lord. I could really understand this. It was hard for me to speak also. I did hear Rachel say to Jesus, "Hello, Master," as though she were acknowledging an old friend. I thought that was interesting. None of them shook His hand or gave Him a hug, which I thought was kind of unusual.

However, as Jesus turned to me, He took hold of both of my hands, and we immediately hugged. As we were doing so, my thought was, "Wow, I'm hugging the Creator Himself, the one who paid the ultimate price for me. We said hello to each other, and I thought, "Wow, what an experience!"

Jesus said, "I have brought you here just like I said I would so that we could talk about your journeys. I know you've been enjoying them, and now you are getting close to completing enough of them so that these all could be placed into book number one. Are you getting excited with what you have completed so far? I want you to know that I am anointing this first volume as well as the remaining three that will come, with my Spirit. Anyone of my brides who reads of your journeys will be greatly encouraged. Just think, others whom the Father has given to Me, but are not mine yet will also read it, for these books will also be used as a tool to reach them. Each will be impacted to be encouraged and drawn to Me. That makes me very excited," He said.

I could tell these words were not simply words but were coming from deep within Him. In other words, He really meant it. I told Him it was my honor to serve Him, and once again I thanked Him for allowing me to do this.

Next, He asked me to walk with Him for a little bit while we talked. I wasn't sure if Dad, Bill, and Rachel would stay there and wait for me to return to where they were standing, but apparently they knew we would not be going too far, so they indicated that they would wait for me to return.

As Jesus and I walked, He wanted me to know just how deeply His love for all of humanity was, but especially those that were already His Bride, as well as those who as yet are not, but will come to acknowledge Him as Lord and Savior. Next, He wanted to instruct me with some matters, of which I am not allowed to discuss, or put into writing at this time. Maybe I will be allowed at a future time, but not for now. Then, He placed His hand in mine, as though He were blessing that which I was doing. Finally, with a big smile on His face, He told me of His love for me and gave me another hug. Then He turned and walked away. I must confess that I didn't want Him to leave, and I just felt numb from the experience.

As I walked back to where my Dad, Bill, and Rachel were standing, I also noticed that Cyberin and the chariot had arrived, so I gave my Dad and Bill a hug goodbye. Then, turning to Rachel, I saw that she had such a sweet smile on her face. She put her arms around my neck and planted a wonderful kiss on my cheek. "It was so good to see you again, Dad," she said. "I just love it when you come. Please come back soon."

Then I climbed into the chariot, waved goodbye to everyone, and we were off. I do not remember anything of the return trip, but I found myself once again sitting in the easy chair in the living room, just thinking about how wonderful both this last trip was along with the first one. This time, I had been gone just nine minutes.

171

Journey Number 48

THE DEPTH OF SPACE

On Tuesday, October 8, 2019, I took another journey. I'm not sure what time it was when I took this trip because I didn't look at the clock before I left, and I didn't look at it immediately upon my return. I do know that this journey was in the middle of the afternoon, sometime around three. Earlier in the week, the Lord spoke to me about taking a trip either on Monday or Tuesday.

So here I was, once again sitting in my comfortable easy chair in the living room, when I thought that now would seem like a good time to go, and so I spoke those all familiar words. "In the name of Jesus, I call for the traveling angel to come and pick me up."

No sooner had I said this than my spirit body left my physical body, and out the front door I went.

As I walked out the front door, I saw Cyberin waiting for me. He gave me a welcome wave, along with his usual big heavenly angelic grin. Then, as I climbed into the chariot, I said hello to him telepathically, and he said, "It's good to see you again, Master Sam." I was surprised to hear him call me Master Sam, for he had never said that to me before.

Before I knew it, we were off, but we didn't head straight north, as he had done before. Quickly entering into outer space, and after climbing for some time, Cyberin took me on a lap around the world so that we could enjoy the beauty of earth, with all of its various colors.

I think that he enjoyed earth's beauty as much as I did. Then after a short lap, he headed the chariot out into space.

I could tell we were heading in a different direction than we had gone previously, so I asked Cyberin where he was taking us. His said the Father wanted me to see another part of His creation.

We traveled first past planets that I recognized within our solar system, then quickly past the sun. Once we were out of our immediate solar system, we were looking at the enormous galaxy, with all of its other planets and stars. That in itself is an amazing site to behold, with its millions and millions of stars, all just glistening in an array of colors.

Before I knew it, we were on the other side of most of them, and Cyberin took me so far out in space that we were actually looking at various clusters of gases that were forming to create stars. There were stars that were just beginning to shine, and as we approached them, Cyberin said it would take several earth years before they would be visible to the naked eye back on the earth. In fact, he said that some would take more than a lifetime from the time that they were created and began to shine before they would become visible to someone looking at them from the earth.

Cyberin then told me that before anything was ever created, there was the Father and space. In other words, space was nothing—just plain darkness. No planets, no stars, not even the Father's home was there. Absolutely nothing! Then the Father decided to create, and He spoke things into Existence. His Home was created for His Glory and pleasure. Then He decided on planets, stars, galaxies, the sun and our solar system. Each piece was created to shine for Him and bring Him praise and glory. He could look out at His creation and enjoy its continued beauty. But He didn't stop there. Just like stars, which have always been forming and shinning, they still, to this day, are continuing to be created and shine for Him. Planets also bring Him praise as He watches how they each continue to fulfill their position under His divine plan, some of which we know about today, and some that have yet to reveal their purpose.

Then Cyberin shocked me with his next statement. "Space, as you know, has no end. It continues to grow until the Father tells it to stop."

I was curious. "Why would it do that?" I asked.

"It's because space in itself brings glory to the Father as it continues to obey His command and grow. By obeying the Fathers command, even though it in of itself has no beauty to speak of, by the mere fact that it continues to obey His command and grow pleases Him. In addition, as He has not yet revealed all of His purposes for these to us, some still remain unanswered. At some time in the future, we will know. This could very well be one." He could see that I was somewhat overwhelmed by the fact that space never ends. I thought there had to be another answer for this that's unknown at the present time.

As we continued to speed through space, Cyberin really surprised me with his comment regarding a black hole, which we could now see, and which appeared to draw space into it, as though it was taking space somewhere else. He told me that it did take it into another level, and he asked me if I wanted him to take us into one so I could see and experience it.

"If we do, are we able to come back?" I said. "And how does that work, since it appears that everything around it is being drawn in and not coming out?"

His said it was just another adventure of the magnitude and mystery of space.

I was curious, but Cyberin could tell that I had some reservations, so he decided that maybe that adventure could be reserved for another journey. I was somewhat relieved to hear him say that.

Cyberin then began turning the chariot in another direction, and it wasn't too long before I could see a huge cluster of stars. They were exquisite in their shinning, and it appeared as though it could have been at the center of space, for as I looked at this array of beauty, it looked like we were looking at a cross road, or an intersection there in space. I thought to myself, could this be what I think it is? Just then, as we came close enough so that I could get a clearer look at things, there in the middle of what appeared to be the center of the crossroads, was the brightest white light. Cyberin must have known what I was thinking. Before I could ask him, he told me that this was the home of the Father, His Son, and all of the redeemed. In other words, as I was looking at this amazing site from space, I was now looking at Heaven itself. Wow, I couldn't believe it. I was actually looking at Heaven from space. It's the actual place where the Father, His Son, and His children now call home.

Cyberin was steering the chariot, and I actually thought he was going to fly in and land somewhere so I could possibly see someone. However, it became obvious to me that it was not to be during this trip. He kind of circled Heaven two times from a distance, and then turned the chariot away from Heaven to head toward the earth for our journey back home.

As we journeyed, he wanted me to know that the direction that we had taken out into space, could be taken in any direction, where the result would be the same. We could have gone to the north, south, east, or west from the earth, and we would have encountered exactly the same results as we had today. Space! Also, the Father wanted me to know just how large space is in any direction. It is absolutely enormous!

Then we returned to earth and the front yard of the house, where I exited the chariot. I thanked Cyberin for the journey. "You've shown me a lot today," I said. "Thank you for the ride." He smiled his big grin, knowing that he had accomplished his mission, and with a wave, he was off, leaving me just standing there in the front yard. After I watched him leave, I turned around and went through the front door, where my spirit body then reentered my physical body that was still sitting in my easy chair, just as I had left it.

As I previously mentioned, I don't know how long that I had been gone, as I had not looked at the clock either before I left or upon my return. All I can say is that upon my return, it was still in the afternoon.

Journey Number 49

FRUIT AND FLOWER &
THE CITY SQUARE

On Tuesday, October 22, 2019, I was sitting in the living room in my comfortable easy chair in the middle of the afternoon. It was 3:33 when I decided that now would be a good time to take a trip. The Lord had told me just a few days earlier that within the next few days I would be traveling once again. It seemed like now would be a good time. I said, "In the name of Jesus, I call for the traveling angel to come and pick me up." Then, up out of the chair I went and out the front door.

There Cyberin was, in the front yard once again. He was wearing his wonderful and welcomed smile on his face. As I approached and started to climb into the chariot, he was the first to speak. "It's good to see you again, Master Sam."

"I'm glad you are here," I said, climbing into the rear of the chariot. "But why did you call me Master Sam?" We had been speaking telepathically, and in just a few brief seconds we were off.

I wasn't sure if he had heard me ask the question or if he was thinking about something else, for he didn't immediately answer me. It wasn't but a brief moment, and then he spoke again. "In Heaven, all are servants, one to another. All of the angels are, as well as each of those with the Fathers seal on them are, while at the same time, everyone views the other as master. It is not the same as we view Jesus the King, but because we are all servants, to us everyone is our master. Therefore, when I come to pick you up and take you to where the Farther wants me to, I am your servant, and you I consider master, because I am serving you, which I'm very pleased to do. Everyone in Heaven is that way, as all are servants to each other, while at the same time each is master as far as the other is concerned. Does that make sense?"

"So, in other words, if I was driving you in the chariot, I would consider myself to be your servant, because I'm serving you. And because you're being served by me, I would also consider you my master, is this correct?"

"Yes," he said. "But you would never serve me, because you have the Father's seal, and I do not, nor will I ever."

We then arrived at our destination in Heaven. As Cyberin brought the chariot to a stop and I stepped out, I thanked him for the ride and the explanation. Then I said, "So much to learn."

He just smiled, gave me a wave goodbye, and off he went. Now I was just standing there alone for a brief moment.

Just then I heard him call my name. "Hello, Sam," he said. "How wonderful to see you again."

Without having to see him, I knew who it was. His voice was deep and strong, and I knew it was Abraham from old. Once he was close enough, we embraced. I was glad to see him.

He instantly made me feel like he wanted to be with me. He gave me his welcome bear hug. He already was a large man, but when he wrapped his arms around me and hugged, without a doubt, I knew I was welcome.

"What would you like to do this trip?" he asked. "Is there some place or someone that you'd like to see?"

I was surprised that he didn't already have an agenda in mind. I told him I wanted to see something that I hadn't seen before. "Okay," he said, "Then let's be off."

He led us in a specific direction, and I wondered just how he would know what all that I'd already seen and how he would know what I hadn't seen yet.

We didn't walk at a pace that would suggest we were heading someplace that required us to be there at a certain time; however, we also were not out for a mere stroll. In addition, since he was a tall man, his stride was larger than mine, and I continually had to pick up my pace just to keep up with him. I very much enjoyed talking with him as we walked. I asked if he remembered living on the earth and how it compared to living here?

His answers were without a doubt very educational for me. He, in turn, wanted to know what it was like for me to travel from earth to Heaven and back in the chariot, and did I ever notice it physically. So the conversation was light, yet informative, and I believe that it was for each one of us. I think I almost floored him when I asked if he liked it here, for his answer was "Are you kidding? Of course I do. This is so much better than being on the earth, or even when I lived in Paradise."

Before I knew it, we came upon an extremely large flower garden. We stopped there, and I could not see from one end to the other. As I looked down the rows, I also was unable to see the end of it, for it appeared to go on for miles in every direction.

The colors were just amazing having colors that I knew from the earth, but as well there were colors, multiples of them that I had never seen before. Without a doubt, this was the most beautiful flower garden I'd ever laid my eyes on. Simply put, it was out of this world, and the fragrance that came from there was well, I don't think I have the adequate words to describe. Every breath seemed to be more and more invigorating. As I would breathe in these various aromas from different flowers, they would add life to me. I could actually feel it recharging my body. Then I realized one of the real reasons that the Farther has uniquely placed flowers all over Heaven. I had to ask Abraham about this. He then told me that this garden had been placed there for two reasons. "First, the Father loves to look at His creation. He enjoys each and every different type of flower. Second, He loves the aroma that each different type of flower produces, and the combined aroma that the combined flowers make together is a sweet aroma to Him. Also, He created these different types of flowers, and each individual fragrance is designed to be nourishing to all that would pass by, wherever they were placed. This is one of the ways that we receive nourishment here in Heaven, through the different fragrances."

When he told me that, I was blown away.

About that time as we were standing there just taking in the scenery, I saw my father-in-law, Merle, walking toward us. It was obvious that he had been out in the fields checking on the flowers.

He kind of half trotted up to the two of us, and with a huge grin on his face, he said, "Hi, Sam. Good to see you again."

We embraced, and I told him that I was so glad to see him, and I wondered whether he knew that Abraham and I would be coming by. He said he did, and while he worked, he kept a look out for us.

"How is everyone on Earth doing?" he asked. "Do me a favor and say hello to my daughters, and Sammy too. Tell them all that I said hello, and that I love them."

I assured him that I would, and then I said, "By the way, have you seen Eck?"

"Oh, yes, many times," he said, laughing. "But I just haven't gotten used to seeing him with hair." We had a good laugh over that one.

"So this is one of the jobs you have here, seeing after these gardens for the Farther," I said.

"Yes," he said, "and I'm both thrilled and honored to do it for Him. I know that He really loves the aromas from all of these. In addition, I get to take them and place them all over the place so others can enjoy them as well.

Merle then led Abraham and me just a few feet to where he had a basket. It was about the size of a bushel basket but made out of something I really didn't look at much because of what was in the basket. Inside were several different kinds of fruit. They were various colors. Merle picked one up. It was about the size of a large apple but had more the shape of a pear. It was golden brown. I remember seeing these on trees that were along the side of the River of Life. Back then, I was told that each of the trees produces twelve different kinds of fruit, each of which had different purposes. Merle now handed it to me. I wasn't sure if I was to examine it or taste it. Both Abraham and Merle encouraged me to take a bite of it, and Merle said it would provide me with a surge of energy. It was all for that, so I took a fairly good size bite, and as I swallowed it, I could actually feel energy flowing through my body. It was a very good feeling, so I took a second and then third bite. It was the same as before, for each time I swallowed, I could actually feel energy charging into and through my body.

I had to ask them what the purpose of the other fruits were, with the different colors.

I was told that one helps you to understand the things and ways of the Father better. Another one was to assist you when you utilize different modes of travel. One was for refreshing your body when you rest.

"So each one has a particular use or purpose," I said.

"Yes," they said. "You will learn more about them as you continue to travel here," Abraham said.

Abraham then indicated that he had one more place that he wanted us to go before I needed to leave, so he felt that we needed to leave. Then I told him that my head was already so full from what I had already seen and heard, and asked him if I could go and then come back for the second half of this trip? He looked puzzled at first, but then said that he understood. Therefore, this trip would be divided into two separate trips, but would be combined as one.

When he said that, I thanked him for understanding. So this would be the first half of trip number 49.

Cyberin approached in the chariot, so I knew that it was time for me to go. I turned to Abraham and thanked him for the time we had spent together, and I gave him an earthly hug, as best I could. Next, turning to my father-in-law, we embraced and I asked him to let my mother-in-law, my dad, my brother Bill, my grandmother, and Rachel know I'd been there. "Please tell them that I love you and all of them, as does Donna, Susie, and Sammy. Then I climbed into the chariot, waved goodbye to them, and we were off.

As I was basking in the thought of what I had just experienced, Cyberin just remained silent, until we landed back in the front yard. As I exited the chariot, he once again waved goodbye, and with the smile on his face, knowing he had accomplished his mission, was off.

I then entered the house, and for a brief few moments sat back down in the easy chair with my physical body. The clock now read 3:50 p.m. I had been gone all of thirteen minutes.

This now begins the second part of journey number 49. It was now 6:37 p.m. on Sunday, November 3, 2019. I had been sitting for just a few moments in my favorite chair, and I thought this seemed like a good time to take the second half of this trip. Therefore, once again, I called for the traveling angel to come and pick me up. Then out the door I went to the front yard, where my chariot and Cyberin were waiting.

We greeted each other with our usual hello, and off we went. I was simply mesmerized by the scenery of space with all of the planets and stars, etc. It is such a breathtaking site that I wish everyone could take this journey, just to see the sights.

Upon our arrival, once again I was greeted by Abraham, who gave me his heavenly hug and said, "Hello, it's good to see you again, Sam." I could tell he was excited to see me and take me to wherever or whatever he had in store, for I could almost feel it in his step as we moved along, somewhat hurriedly.

We traveled by foot this time, and in a short while we arrived in what I would describe as a city square. At first, I thought we'd be heading toward the throne plaza area, but we didn't. This, however, was an entirely different area of Heaven and somewhat in a different direction from where we'd landed and I thought we would be heading.

As we began walking into the city square, I noticed the structures, which seemed to have similar construction materials. For lack of a better word, I will just call the materials heavenly. The buildings were all the same color, and some structures were taller than others. However, Abraham kept us walking into the center of the square. I hadn't had much time to continue to look around when we arrived in the center square area. That's when Abraham stopped me, and as he did, he pointed to a square that was right in the center of the area, but as he pointed it out to me, I noticed that it had a golden circle in the middle of it. It looked like a golden ring and I estimated that it was between twelve inches and eighteen inches in diameter. He then told me that it had special significance to it and instructed me to step right on it. As I began to move toward it, I notice others stopping and looking at me, I guess to catch my reaction to what was about to happen.

When I stepped on the circle, instantly I was able to see so much of what was going on in Heaven, all at the same time. I could see worship and singing, working and teaching, laughing, listening, all in an instant and at the very same time. It was as though I was there myself with each event. It was simply amazing.

I was not only able to see many events going on in Heaven at the same time, but was also able to see much of what was presently going on the earth. This included not only current or present events but past history events as well. Then to my amazement, I was also able to see future events both in Heaven and the earth. Everything was done simultaneously.

As I was standing there watching in amazement, I thought of the four living creatures in the throne room in Revelation chapter four, which had eyes all over them, with their ability to see all things taking place everywhere. Then Abraham told me that much of what I was experiencing, that everyone who comes here is this way, or has this ability. As a result, they know much more than they could possibly know when they were on the earth. I could only stand there on the circle for just a few brief moments, as I felt like my head was about to explode. Feeling that way, I needed to step off of the circle to somewhat regain my composure.

I asked Abraham if everyone has the ability here to be able to take all of this material and knowledge in at the same time. He explained that not only do the redeemed have the ability but the angels as well. I was simply blown away and said, "Wow!"

Then he told me that experiencing this was his assignment for me for this trip, and it was time that he brought me back to where Cyberin had dropped me off. So we started to walk back but on the way I asked him if the knowledge ever increases or decreases with different individuals. He said, "Yes, it all depends on what the Father wants each one to know." With that explanation, I somewhat understood.

We arrived back at our starting point, and Cyberin was already there. I thanked Abraham for the experience and tried to give him a big hug goodbye but to no avail. He's just that big a guy. However, I think he knew my intentions. We waved goodbye and were off.

Soon I found myself sitting back in the easy chair just trying to reflect on what I had just experienced. The clock now read 7:02 p.m. Just twenty-five minutes had elapsed.

Journey Number 50

THE ENCOUNTERS

It was Sunday evening, November 24, 2019, and late enough that I had been thinking about going to bed. I wasn't sure what time it was because I had not thought about taking a trip. I had been spending some time in prayer when the Lord spoke to me about my next trip. He said, "As you journey during this next trip, I want you to meet and interview ten different people. As you interview them, you will see that not only are they from different places on the earth, but they are also from different times. I want you to ask them what they remember regarding their life on the earth, their journey here, and how they have enjoyed being here. You will know who you are to interview, as I have already put everything in motion. Therefore, you will not have to search for them."

Needless to say, I was excited, and cautiously optimistic with this assignment.

On Wednesday, November 27, 2019, at 2:17 p.m., the house was quiet, and I was sitting once again in my easy chair in the living room, and I thought that now would be a good time for a journey to start the assignment. I said, "In the name of Jesus, I call for the traveling angel to come and pick me up." Then, just like before, my spirit body left my physical body still sitting in the chair, and out the front door my spirit body went to an awaiting chariot and driver there just waiting for me in the front yard. As I climbed into the chariot, Cyberin greeted me with his usual large grin.

As we took off, he said to me, "You have a huge task on you this trip, Master Sam, but I think you'll really enjoy interviewing all of those people. I wish that one day the Father would ask me to do something like that. But I know why He is assigning you this task, for as some on the earth will read about what you will write, they will also be encouraged."

We appeared to be traveling at a high rate of speed, so I could not just sit back and enjoy the view, and before I knew it, we were there.

As we came to our destination and Cyberin brought the chariot to a stop, I thanked him for the quick journey and stepped out. Then he was off, and I found myself standing there all by myself. However, this place was new to me. I realized that I was not in a place that we had been to before. As I looked around, I noticed a building that looked like it could be a worship center or meeting building, and I noticed many people standing out in the front of it, so I decided to head in that direction. I was about half of the way there, when I had my first encounter.

"Hi, Sam," he said. "I've been waiting around looking for you. I knew you were coming."

How did he know was my thought? I had to remind myself that this was Heaven.

He introduced himself as Rudy or Ruby. I wasn't sure of the correct spelling, because he had a heavy accent. He told me he'd lived on the earth during the fifteenth century. He had lived in Europe and had been killed during a war. I was surprised that he remembered that.

"So, you have been here for well over five hundred years," I said.

He said he wouldn't know. He had no idea of time, for time was not a factor there.

Then he told me that he just loved being here, that he had met King Jesus many times, and that he loved serving others wherever and whenever he can. Then he surprised me when he told me that

186

he loved exploring different parts of Heaven. He had not seen all of it but was continually searching its wonders.

He said, "Everyone should come here for this is such a wonderful place." He then told me that the Father has created a lovely home for him and invited me to come and see it with him. He told me that he is never bored here, and that there was always so much to do. He said, "He just loves it here." Also, that he has many friends here both human and angelic.

I was thinking about going with him to see his home and what his community was like when I had my second encounter. As we were standing there, another stranger came up to us and introduced himself as Sebastian. At the time I wasn't sure if the two of them knew each other, but then, as they shook hands, I could tell that this also was their first meeting.

Sebastian told us that he was born in 1860, and he remembered seeing many changes taking place while he was on the earth. He told me he'd died at the old age of seventy-seven but would never forget how the Father had sent an angel to come and get him.

He must have known that what I really wanted to know about was his life here in Heaven, because he then said he just loved it there, and if possible he would encourage for everyone that he could to come here. He said, "It's so much better than living on the earth. There's so much to see and do here, you would just love it." Then he wanted me to come with him so he could show me the house that the Father had created just for him. He also confirmed that he has met King Jesus many times, and that he just loves spending time with him. I was somewhat taken back when he said that he just loves it when everyone begins praising the Lord all together. He said he'd never felt anything like that while on the earth.

I thought I could possibly see both of their houses, so we started walking together in one direction. I assumed both men lived in the same general direction, and I felt their houses must not have been too far, as we began walking rather than flying.

I wanted to know more, so I asked them about life here, as opposed to life on the earth. Both men had large smiles on the faces, and I assumed that both of them must have been thinking about something in particular that they would have recalled.

We hadn't walked but a little way when a woman approached. Just like the two men, she appeared to be in her early thirties. She said, "Hello, Sam," as if we were old friends. I said hello back to her, and she greeted both Rudy/Ruby and Sebastian. I could tell they were not familiar with each other, but I must confess that the heavenly greeting is much more genuine than the greeting on the earth.

She then told us that her name was Leanne. I could tell that she was an intelligent woman. She was not a pretty woman but not ugly either. However, when she spoke about Jesus, her eyes just lit up. She said she lived quite a distance from the throne, so when she goes there, she enjoys flying there all the time. She said that she just loves being in His presence. She indicated that she'd been there not quite sixty earth years and originally was from England.

I wanted to know more, so I asked her if she remembered coming here to Heaven. Her answer kind of gripped me, as she told the three of us men how she had been physically abused and killed by her husband when she was in her late twenties. She said she remembered that during her last minutes alive on Earth, she saw an angel come for her, and he helped her travel from Earth to Heaven. She didn't remember much of the first minutes after arriving in Heaven, except that she felt a peace that she had not felt while alive on the earth.

Of course, she wanted me to come and see the house that the Father had designed and built just for her. To me this appeared to be a usual theme from those that I had encountered thus far. I wanted to ask her about her life here in Heaven, but I saw Cyberin and the chariot coming, so I knew that my time was limited.

I asked all three of them if there was one thing they could all agree on about Heaven. The answer was the same from each of them. Worshipping here was unlike anything they'd ever experienced on the earth. Also, this place was filled with joy, peace, and love that knows no limits. All three of them appeared to be in their early thirties.

I thanked them for their time and climbed into the chariot with Cyberin. I was thinking this journey was over and that I'd be going back to the earth. However, I was quite wrong, for as Cyberin and I left the area and waved goodbye, he turned the chariot toward another destination, which didn't take very long to get to.

As we were coming in to land, I could see that two men were standing there just waiting for us. The chariot came to a stop, and I began to climb out. The two men greeted me. "Hello, Sam," they said at the same time, as if we had known each other for quite a long time. However, they were new to me. We had never met before. As we shook hands, I asked them how they knew that I would be coming, when I would be coming to, and just where I would be arriving at. Their answer was the same as others who had answered that question for me before. They said, "We just know."

I had to remind myself that this was Heaven, and things here were much different than on the earth. Knowing the answers to my question was obviously one of those things.

Next, they introduced themselves as the brothers, Jason and Peter. They told me they had both died in an automobile accident in 2012. They were both in their late teens at the time and had lived with their parents in Indianapolis, Indiana.

As I looked at them, I couldn't help but notice that even though they were late teenagers at the time of their arrival here in Heaven, which by the way was only seven years ago, yet now they looked much more mature and appeared to be around the age of most everyone else here, in their early thirties.

Peter told me he was the older of the two of them by a little over one earth year, and he did most of the talking by far, so I kind of turned my attention to him. I wanted to know what he came here to tell me. The first thing he talked about was that he and his brother didn't live together but lived next door to each other. Also, they didn't live in large homes but in something that on the earth would be similar to a condo. I thought that was interesting, but I was assured that they both just love the situation the Father had created just for them and felt that it was very special. I was glad to hear that.

Next, I wanted to know if they'd come first to paradise, or did they arrive right into Heaven? Their answer was that they came right into Heaven. Peter said that since they had both grown up in the church, while they were there, they had experienced some of being in the presence of God.

"In other words," I said, "age may be a small factor in whether you arrive first into paradise, or Heaven, but having an ongoing relationship with the Father and His Son Jesus, and experiencing some of His presence appeared to me to be more of where you go when you first arrive here." They both just smiled and agreed.

"So what is it that the two of you do here all day?" I said. Peter told me he was an outdoorsman, and he loved going to various places, including the mountains, rivers, lakes, and even the snowy white caps. Then he surprised me when he told me he had heard that I had gone fishing with Jesus and that he has yet to do that, but wanted to. Jason on the other hand was a book worm, and he had a huge appetite for all things written. He said it was one of his passions while he was on the earth, and obviously the Father has let that still be his passion while he is here. I thought that it was interesting that some of what you were like on the earth will still be you here in Heaven. His passion also included continuing the study of God's Word. He said that much of what you would think would not apply here in Heaven still did. I thought that was interesting. However, without any doubt, both men said the thing they enjoyed the most was when a large group of humans or angels gathered around the throne and just entered into worship. Jason said that without any doubt, to him, this was the ultimate highlight. Then he said, "I'm so excited when I think that I will be able to do this for all of eternity well it's just amazing for me to think about. I always look forward to this time."

Peter agreed with his brother, offering an astounding yes.

Peter said he loved exploring Heaven. He said that while he knew he hasn't been there for very long, he wanted to see all that he can of his new home. "It's such an interesting place. There's always something new to see and do here," he said.

Just then Cyberin flew in with the chariot, so I knew that my time with these two men was about up. I thanked them for their time and said I'd like to come back sometime and sit down with them to discover what additional things they had learned or discovered. They assured me that they would like that also. I then climbed into the chariot, waved goodbye, and Cyberin and I were off. I had no idea if we were heading somewhere else for another encounter or if he were taking me back to the front yard to my home on the earth. I decided to just sit back and see what developed. Cyberin must have read my thoughts, for I heard him giggle a little.

We traveled for what seemed like only a few seconds, and Cyberin started to bring us in for a landing, so I knew we were not heading back to the earth but that he was taking me to yet an additional place for another encounter. As we came to the place he was heading, we stopped in the front of someone's home. I couldn't help but wonder just who lived there. I imagined that possibly a general or polititian lived there, for the home was meticulously maintained and had the appearance of a colonial type home. However, as Cyberin stopped the chariot, and as I was exiting it, I saw that a gentleman was walking out of the front door. Obviously, he was the next person that I was to interview.

As we started to walk toward each other, I heard him say, "You must be Sam. I've been looking forward to meeting you and speaking with you." He introduced himself as Mike or Mikey, and he indicated that when he was on the earth, he had lived in Australia. His accent was so pronounced that it was somewhat difficult to understand him. I asked him his name again. He said the identical thing, so I just elected to leave it at that.

I asked him to tell me somethings about himself.

"I lived at the turn of the nineteenth century and that he had drowned at sea. He remembered that as he was drowning, an angel had come right down into the sea and picked him up. He remembered going through a tunnel on his journey here that had many lights, however they had traveled so fast that he was not able to stop and look at all of those lights. Now he'd been here for over a hundred earth years but didn't remember much about his former life.

He told me that upon his arrival here, the first person he'd met here was Jesus. He said that he'd never forget that first encounter. "It was so special. I could not get over meeting Him. When I first saw Him and recognized who He was, I could not help myself, and we hugged. He was such a good friend. I have had several visits with Him since then, and they are very special to me. But I must tell you that when He looks at you, it doesn't matter where you are or what you're doing, it's as though He can see right through you. I just love Him, and I always enjoy our times together.

"When we first met, He took me to the great meeting hall. As we entered, and those who were already there realized the Jesus had just entered, I heard people saying, 'The Master is here,' and an enormous cheer erupted. We began walking through the entrance, and Jesus led us through rows and rows of tables, chairs and people and eventually, He brought us to my place in the room. As we stopped, I looked at the table and found my name permanently etched into the table. This was to be my place in the great hall for all of eternity, and I've never forgotten that."

He then told me that since being here, he'd met wonderful friends and relatives who had gone before him, as well as some who'd come after, and he talked about how he has enjoyed the great reunion. However, he indicated that by far, what brings him the most enjoyment is worshipping the lord with other saints. Also, he said, "Meeting with others to discuss the goodness of the Father is a wonderful highlight here."

Since he had drowned in his former life, I was curious to find out about his relationship with water. I had to ask him. His response surprised me. He told me he had been out on the water many times, that he really enjoyed walking on the water, and that there was no need for a boat here. He also said he enjoyed walking in the water and is fascinated with being able to go down under to the underwater adventures.

My time with him was just about up. I watched Cyberin and the chariot arriving. I thanked him for his time and said I would like to come back again to learn more from him. I then indicated that if I did, that perhaps then he could show me the inside of his home. As I climbed into the chariot, we shook hands, waved good bye and Cyberin and I were off. I wondered to where.

His name was Steven. He was next on the list for me to meet. He loved music and played in a band during high school. Guitar was his passion, but he kind of lost it when he and his parents moved from the lower part of Canada to the extreme northern area of Canada. As he got older, he lived alone in a small, one-room house with only a wood-burning stove for heat. He told me that one night, when it was extremely cold outside, he'd fallen asleep and forgotten to load the stove with wood. As a result, he froze to death. The year was 1771. At the time, he was twenty-nine earth years old.

At the time of his death, he remembered hearing Jesus call his name. The next thing he knew, there he was, just standing in

Heaven. He had accepted Jesus Christ as his Savior when he was a small boy. He told me how great a joy it was when his mom and dad came to greet him as he arrived there in Heaven. They were the very first to meet him. He hadn't seen them for several years, as they had both died earlier, his Dad, twenty-seven years before, and his Mom just twelve years before he did.

I asked Steven if he had been waiting very long for Cyberin and me and the chariot to come. He said he knew we were coming soon, so he just stood around waiting and looking for our arrival. He told me that he hadn't seen to many chariots, and none in fact up close, so he said that he thought that it would be interesting to see us coming. Then he told me that during his days on the earth, they called a horse drawn buggy a chariot. We had a good laugh over that one. I was curious about why he would find this chariot interesting, when now Steven traveled as fast as lightning or by thought. Steven said that one day he wanted to take a ride in the chariot. He thought it would just be interesting to do.

"So, you have been here for well over two hundred years," I said. "But you don't look a day over thirty, perhaps thirty-three. What's your secret?"

He just laughed and told me that here, no one ages once they get to this certain age. He said that here they all refer to it as the perfect age, which was all designed by the Father. When he said that I thought, "He's almost 250 earth years old, yet he looks younger than me. How cool is that?"

I wanted to know more about where he lived, how far from the throne it was, and did he fly much when he moved around. He told me the Father knew what would give him joy as He was creating his home, so the Father knew he not only loved having a place in the city, where lots of people where, but he also knew he loved being out in the wooded mountains, and so the Father built him a second home in the mountains that he could go to whenever he wanted. He said when he went there, he always flew or traveled by thought. He said that traveling by thought is so much faster than flying, but sometimes he just liked to fly there just so he could enjoy the view. I understood what he was saying about being in the city, as I had noticed that when Cyberin and I had left Mike or Mikey to come to where Steven was, we had not traveled for very long.

Next I asked Steven what he thought of this place.

"Oh, you'll never get tired of it here. There's always something to do. It's a great place. After being here for a while, I'd never want to go back to living on the earth. This place will definitely spoil you."

Then he really shocked me when he told me about one of the most enjoyable things he'd found here. He said, "I don't know if you've noticed it yet, but the love here is everywhere. It is without a doubt in everybody, and I just think it is wonderful. I believe that it originates from the Father because of His love for each one of us. Therefore, you can't help but receive it as well as give it at the same time. The love that each one has for the other is a form of praise to the Father, which He has designed that way."

This was and still is most important to the Father. He said it was to him as well. I could not help but be moved and encouraged. I told him I would do my best to take that message back with me to the earth.

I wanted to know more, but Cyberin approached. Steven saw him before I did and said, "Look, here comes your ride." I thanked Steven for the time we had spent. Before I got into the chariot, Steven grabbed a hold of my arm and gave me a big hug. He wasn't a very large man, but his hug showed me just how big his heart was. Then I climbed into the chariot and sat down. Steven put both of his hands on the chariot, indicating that he wanted to look around a bit. Cyberin was patient with him, and when he was done, we all smiled and waved goodbye to each other, and we were off once again. Now I was beginning to enjoy these quick visits, but I wished I had a little more time for additional questions.

We traveled for what seemed a longer period than we had ever before. It was like we were traveling around the world, but we finally came down in a small community. As we landed in what I would call the city square, there, off to my left, was a gentleman sitting on a park bench. I noticed that as I was stepping out of the chariot, he waved, arose from the bench, and started walking the short distance to Cyberin and me.

When he got close enough, he introduced himself as Nigel, and he said that he had been there waiting for just a little while as he knew that we were coming soon.

As I reached out to shake his hand, he looked at me somewhat strangely, and he didn't reach out to shake mine. Then he caught himself, as though he remembered something, and he grabbed hold of my hand to begin shaking it. He said he'd only been there a few earth days and had lived with a paralyzed arm and hand for many years while he was on the earth, so he was still just getting used to having a fully functioning right arm again. I assured him that I understood and said that there appeared to be many things different here than on the earth.

We watched as Cyberin departed in the chariot, and we continued watching until he was completely out of sight. Nigel told me he just could not get over traveling like that, and I assured him that he was going to be blown away as he learns the different modes of transportation here, that traveling by an angel driven chariot being the slowest one. When I said that, I noticed a puzzled look on his face.

I asked him about his departure from the earth. I wanted to know what if anything he remembered.

He said he didn't remember much, except that while he was on the earth, he had been sick for quite a while. He didn't remember the journey there, but he remembered his first moments here as he arrived, and he commented about people he didn't know, who kept coming up to him and welcoming him. He said he couldn't get over how friendly everyone here was and how love just seemed to flow from everyone that he meets.

I asked him if he had made it to the throne area yet, or the great meeting building. I was somewhat surprised by his answer, which was no. It was interesting to me that since I had taken several journeys here already, that I was more familiar with Heaven than he was, for I felt like he was not going to be telling me about this place, but that I was able to tell him about some things that he would yet experience.

Nigel told me he was in his late forties when he died, but now he felt like he was much younger, and he felt he was much healthier than when he was on the earth. I told him that he looked like a man in his thirties, maybe younger. He said he felt really alive.

He'd been a coal miner in his earlier days while living in Pennsylvania, and had developed a lung problem, which is why he had been sick for such a long time. He told me that one of the first things he noticed when he arrived here was his ability to breathe deeper and freely.

I asked him what he wanted to do here, and he said that he hadn't seen Jesus yet, and was really looking forward to doing that. He said others he'd spoken with since he had arrived had assured him that he would. He didn't feel worthy, because he had only become a Christian for just a short while. I told him that didn't matter, but what was important was that he had accepted Jesus Christ as his Savior. That was the important part. I said if he hadn't, he wouldn't even have made it here. He smiled, wiped his forehead, and said "Whew. Glad I made the right choice."

I asked if there was something he also wanted or didn't want to do here. His answer made me laugh. He didn't want to work down in the coal mines again. I assured him that there are no coal mines here in Heaven.

I could see that Cyberin had already landed, so we started walking toward him. I thanked Nigel for his time and welcomed him here. Then I told him that he was just at the beginning of a wonderful time here with other saints, loved ones, and friends. I said, "Everyone continues to confirm to me just how wonderful the Father has made this place for His children, including you."

He smiled, we waved goodbye, and Cyberin and I were off.

He lived during the eleventh century, during the days of slavery. He told me his name was Moses and that he didn't know exactly where he was from. He knew he was brought up in a slave camp and worked on a farm raising different kinds of vegetables. He was one of five children. They never had much of anything, including their own house. Someone had told him once that he lived in Europe, but where in Europe he didn't know.

I had met Moses shortly after Cyberin and I had said goodbye to Nigel. When we left Nigel, we had not flown too far, and now we'd landed in a black community. Moses was the first black man I had ever met or even seen before in Heaven, and this was my very first excursion into a community such as this. Not that there was anything wrong with it, mind you, but up until that point in my journeys, I had not had the privilege before.

When we landed, several folks from the community came up to see the chariot. I guess it had not been a usual event, so they were curious to look at it. Also, they didn't seem curious to see me, which I found interesting.

Moses stepped out of the group and introduced himself and told me he was the man that I was to see here. I was still sitting in the chariot at the time, and we shook hands while I was still sitting there, and as some of the others started to walk away, I exited the chariot. After I did, the two of us just stood there and watched as Cyberin and the chariot flew off.

As I looked around and saw that I was the only Caucasian in this sea of black saints, I felt a little unusual. However, they were all very friendly to me, and I continued to greet those that had come with Moses and had stayed. I wondered if I was going to interview just Moses or the group that had gathered together. There were six including Moses, so I decided to begin my interview with him.

"Do you remember when you died and how you died?" I asked.

He told me that because of the working and living conditions, he remembered that he had been sick for a long time. "But you didn't get paid unless you worked, so I had to, even though I was sick. Eventually I got so sick that I couldn't work anymore, and eventually, I died." He said that when he'd been a small child, his momma used to sing spiritual songs to him and tell him about Jesus. He told me she had led him to the Lord when he was twelve. He said he stayed true to the Lord for the rest of his life, until he died, but he didn't know how old he was when he died.

I told him he'd been here in Heaven for well over eight hundred earth years. He seemed very surprised.

I asked him about his living conditions, and he said that when he'd come here, the Father had built a home for him, and the Father knew that his dream of a lifetime was to one day own his own home. He told me that his mother, wife, and two of his five children all live close by in the same community.

I asked him if he liked being here, as compared to living on the earth, and he told me that he liked it here so much better. He said he really liked the love that everyone has for each other here. He said that he was sure that it first starts from the Father. Also, he said that the angels are very kind and will do anything for you. "Just gathering together with neighbors and worshipping the Lord is something that I always enjoy. It's the richest thing here," he said.

I then asked him if there was any prejudice here, and he looked at me funny and asked what that was. By his expression, I knew that I had my answer. I asked him whether there was anything there that he didn't like to do. He said no.

I then asked him if we could take a little walk so that I could meet his family, but by that time I could see Cyberin and the chariot coming back, so I said, "Perhaps another time."

He asked if I were going to go back to the earth soon, and he asked me what earth year it would be. I told him it was 2019.

"Wow," he said.

As I shook his hand and thanked him for the brief time that we'd spent, he said he had a question for me. He was wondering if I could take a message back with me for everyone who's alive on the earth now. I told him that the Father would have to approve of it, but that he should go ahead and give it to me now.

"Please tell everyone that Heaven is real, that there are many brothers and sisters here already who are doing just fine, and for each one to not miss the opportunity to come here."

I thanked him and waved goodbye, and Cyberin and I were off.

As Cyberin and I approached the park, I noticed a man standing under one of the trees. He appeared to be just watching us as we came in for a landing. He walked over to where we were and said good morning to us. I was stepping out of the chariot on the right side, and he approached on the left. I walked around behind the chariot to meet him. His smile was infectious, and he looked like he was in his early thirties. He had dark black hair that went down to just about his shoulder, and he had dark eyes. Also, his complexion was a dark olive color.

He told me his name was Jake and that when he had lived on the earth, he had lived in Argentina. He had died at the age of twelve. He said that he'd been climbing in a large tree and had fallen and had hit his head. He'd died instantly. I could tell he had remembered it well, for he spoke of the incident in colorful detail. I then asked him if he knew what year that was, and he told me that it was 1727. I told him that, based on what he had just said, he had been here for just under three hundred earth years.

I asked him if he remembered much about living on the earth, or if he remembered how he got here. He said that he didn't remember much about his childhood, but he did remember that his parents took him to a Catholic church every week, and he was an altar boy.

He said it was during this time that he learned about Jesus Christ, and at eleven, he prayed a prayer to accept Him as his Savior.

He told me about the time he'd fallen out of the tree and hit his head. An angel came and picked him up in his arms and carried him to Heaven. He said that at the time, he thought the ride with the angel was cool.

He said that when he first arrived, he was still so young and that he was taught about the ways of God by certain other people that were there to do the teaching. He said that eventually he grew up to the person that was now standing before me.

I wanted to encourage him to tell me something I could take back with me to the earth, but I didn't want to try and force it out of him, so I asked him what it has been like for him here.

His answer surprised me. "This place is wonderful, and there is always something to do here."

I asked him what his favorite thing to do here was.

"Oh, I just love to go along the river of life and encourage others to sample the different kinds of fruit. Why do you ask?"

I told him that I had been there before and had tasted a couple, but not all of them. He said that there are several types, each of which do have different uses. He said one was for energy, another for wisdom, while still another helped you to know more or understand more about the Father.

I asked if he had made many friends here, and you could have knocked me over with a feather.

"Yes, and one of them is, in fact, your brother Bill. Oh, we're good friends. When Bill first came here, one of my jobs was to show him some of the mountains. Bill now tells me that has become one of his favorite things to do." He said Bill and he went to the mountains quite frequently. Bill liked it there, just like I do. Then he told me that the next time he saw Bill, he'd let him know he'd seen me. I thought this was just like the Father, to save this last interview with someone who not only knew my brother but did things with him as well, even though he had been there in Heaven for over two hundred earth years.

As we were talking about Bill, Cyberin approached, so I knew it was time for me to leave. I also knew that this interview with Jake was my tenth or last interview, for now I had completed the Fathers assignment. That meant that when Cyberin and I were going to leave, he would be taking me back to my home on the earth.

As I started to climb into the chariot, Jake thanked me for coming and invited me to come back. I turned around, and Jake and I hugged. As I then sat down in the chariot, Jake said to tell everyone that I meet on Earth hello for him.

We all waved goodbye, and I just sat back in my seat in the chariot and enjoyed the short ride back. However, as we were heading back to Earth, Cyberin asked me if I had enjoyed the assignment. I told him I really had.

He said, "I knew that you would."

Back on the earth in the front yard, I exited the chariot, and as I looked back at Cyberin, he had his usual grin on his face. He then gave me a wave goodbye and was off. I went inside of the house to my waiting physical body, still sitting in the easy chair.

HEAVEN IS THE PLACE TO BE

I dream of Heaven, oh what a place
If I could see Jesus face to face
I've read in a Book, others who have seen,
Of people and beauty, of Glory to glean.
I prayed to the Lord with all of my heart,
Would you pick me, from this world to depart!

He answered and said, "My son you can go"
For things I will show you, you didn't even know
Sitting in my chair, I could hardly believe
An angel was there, it was now time to leave

With door opened wide, what did I see?
A beautiful chariot prepared just for me!
I went and I sat and upward we went
Where were we going, I knew what it meant.

The things I've seen, no words can express
It's peace, love, and joy, and free from all stress.

All of a sudden, while standing in place
I saw crowds of people, who would I face
To my surprise, A man came near,
He said, "I'll show around, you have nothing to fear

Behold, it was Abraham, the prophet of old
He showed me the mansions and things of gold

Standing in awe of this beautiful place,
I turned to my left and saw His Face.

All of a sudden my eyes filled with tears,
I hit the Floor, there were never any fears.

Now standing tall, He said to me…
I've much for you to do and many to see.

His shoulder length hair, dark Brown was the shade
Small Beard and Mustache, never to fade.
His Eyes so beautiful, His Face all a Glow,
With Smile so Infectious, His Peace He did show.

His White Robe flowing such Joy He brings,
Wearing a Purple Sash which reads;
King of Kings.

Another surprise was in store for me
Someone calling my name, who would it be?
It's my father-in-law who said, "heard you were here"
Just had to see you since you were so near

He was young and handsome, oh what a sight,
With his white robe flowing, he could take to flight
"How are my daughters, he came to say
Tell them we're praying for them, come what may."

One more sight for my eyes to behold,
much more precious than silver and gold
My father running toward me, oh what joy
He threw his arms around me, his little boy.

His eyes so blue and his hair so fine
What a beautiful sight this father of mine.

No one can imagine the times I've had
The beauty I've seen and never to be sad.

Forever it will be etched in my heart
What an awesome place, it's hard to depart
Thank you Lord for taking me there
My memories to keep and someday to share!

By Susie B.

THE STILL SMALL VOICE:
A PERSONAL WORD

H ave you ever had an experience so strange, so unusual, that it totally revolutionizes and changes your whole life?

This is a true life experience that has literally transformed my life. Because of the impact it has made on me, I've felt led to write my story for your benefit. I've dedicated it to those of you who can identify with some of the same experiences in this story.

Sam Radobenko

L ike most people, I had always figured that each man's fate was in his own hands. What we got out of life, I thought, was directly proportionate to what we put into it. With that in mind, in 1975, at the age of twenty-five, I began my own roofing business and attempted to make my mark in the world.

My success was nearly immediate. In less than two years, I took a company with zero net worth and built it into a firm worth in excess of $200,000. With eighteen people in production, my income went from $4.50 per hour to over $10,000 per month. I had, without a doubt, become successful. In fact, I'd become too successful. With office personal doing their job, salespeople, and a production supervisor handling the production, I was free of responsibility by ten o'clock each morning. Bored, I began to take up "rich man's hobbies," like golf, toys, and drinking. Within a year, I was downing a quart of hard whiskey a day—six quarts a week. When that wasn't enough, I turned to drugs—marijuana, uppers, downers, cocaine—anything I could use to find the ultimate high. While I honestly believe I wasn't an addict or an alcoholic, I do know that I certainly was not satisfied with my life.

There's a saying in Texas, where I was living at the time: "You aren't known in Texas until you've been shot at once, but if you've been shot at twice, it's time to leave." Shortly after I had obtained what I thought was a high level of success, I did become "known," and soon after, it also became "time for me to leave."

Driving down a Texas interstate one day, I approached a car attempting to merge from an entrance ramp. Slowing down to allow this other car to complete its maneuver, I was greeted with a somewhat obnoxious honk from a van behind me. Obviously irate, the van's driver pulled out from behind me and accelerated until his van was abreast of my car. Glancing over at the other driver in a totally nonconfrontational way, I was amazed to see that he'd pulled out a .45. More horrifying was the fact that he began firing at me. One of the slugs blew a tire, and as he sped away, I caught the van's license plate number. Angered, I limped to the nearest exit, where I found a phone and called the law.

They responded immediately and were able to apprehend the culprit some ten miles down the road. When asked why he'd shot at me, the driver shrugged and said he'd been angered by the fact that I'd slowed down. This man had no vendetta to settle; we'd never met each other.

It was only a few months later that the second shooting took place. Every Thursday, I typically stayed at the office all night long. This would allow me to catch up on any unfinished business that needed my attention and would ensure that I wouldn't be interrupted as I worked.

One week, for no particular reason, I decided that instead of working, I would go home. When I came in Friday morning, I was stunned to see that my office looked like the target at a firing range. The windows were shot out, and there were bullets embedded in my desk and chair. I counted seven rounds in furniture, which, if I'd stayed the night before, could have ended in me. Retrospectively I realize I'd been protected from fatal harm in both of these instances. At the time I called it luck. Now I know better.

Shortly after the second shooting incident, I took my Blazer and went hunting with a friend. Attempting to ford a wash that was filled with water, I sank the Blazer, necessitating a complete engine overhaul. Another friend, who lived in Big Springs, a town some forty miles from where I lived, agreed to repair the truck for me, so I took it over and left it with him. After about three months, he called and said it was finally ready, so I made arrangements to go and pick it up.

I asked a trusted employee, Stan, to go to Big Springs with me in a pickup and drive the truck on the return trip. Stan was more than just an employee; he was a good friend, drinking buddy, and as loyal as the day was long. I'd never asked anything of Stan and been refused, and this proved to be no exception. This trip, however, set the stage for Stan's first denial to me, but that will come later.

The trip to Big Springs was uneventful. We picked up the Blazer and headed home. I was in the lead in the Blazer, and Stan was following me in the pickup. As I drove, I wore my headphones, a necessity because of the roar of the oversized tires on the Blazer. Grooving to the music, I thought of little more than how happy I was to have the Blazer back.

We were only about five miles out of Big Springs when, for no apparent reason, I reached down and pulled the tape out the stereo and took my headphones off. I'd no sooner done this than I heard a voice call my name. Startled, I looked around, but there was no one in the cab with me. Before I could ponder the situation, I heard someone call my name again.

There's no way to describe the voice. It was full of power, and yet, at the same time, unbelievably gentle. It was accompanied by a strange fragrance—sweeter and more beautiful than roses. A third time the voice called, and still I had no idea what was happening. Suddenly, I got very excited as I realized that it was the Lord speaking to me.

As I drove along, it became obvious that, though I was sitting in the driver's seat, I no longer had control of the Blazer. Staring out the windshield, I could see the hood of the Blazer and the road, but they both were encompassed in what appeared to be a tunnel,

213

surrounded by a big cloud. As I continued on, the Lord told me He loved me and that there wasn't much time left before His return. He went on to say that there was much work yet to be done.

It was at that point that He asked me a most important question. "Sam, are you happy with your life?"

Interestingly enough, I'd never asked myself that question before. With success surrounding me, you would think I'd have every reason on earth to be happy. Yet, I wasn't. Upon close examination, I realized that I wasn't actually happy but that I didn't have any complaints either. Pondering only a moment, I responded that while I wasn't happy, I didn't see anything wrong with the worldly highs I was experiencing.

"You're a man who deals with the facts," the Lord said. "So, let's look at where you are today and where you're going and what I have to offer."

As he spoke, I visualized a sheet of paper with a line drawn down the center. One side was labeled "Your Way" and the other side, "God's Way."

While this was fixed in my mind's eye, the Lord asked me the first of three all important questions. "Sam, who makes all of the decisions in your life? In your business life? In your personal affairs, who makes the decisions?"

Because of my position in life, I had, of course, made all my own decisions, whether I wanted to or not.

Without waiting for a reply, the Lord continued. "How would you like Me to make all of those decisions for you? How would you like it if, when you didn't want to make a decision, you could just hand it over to the decision-making department and not have to worry about it? That's what I can do for you."

That might not sound like too big of a deal to you, but like so many others, I had reached the point where I was tired of making all the tough decisions in life. Therefore, I chalked one up for God on the balance sheet.

Taking somewhat of a different approach, the Lord then asked, "Sam, the drugs, the alcohol—why do you use them?"

Somehow, I knew all the excuses were not going to cut it with the Lord, for the truth was that I, like everyone else, was hiding behind the drugs and alcohol because I didn't want to face the real issues of life that were before me, and I liked the numbness that the highs provided me.

"Sam," the Lord said. "I'll give you highs that are ten times greater than anything you have ever experienced."

At the time, I wasn't sure I could handle that. Needless to say, however, I was sure willing to try. Check number two went to God's side of the balance sheet.

As I was basking in the thought of this "ultimate high," the Lord brought me back to a more sober state with a final question. "Sam, if I were to come today, or if your life were to end today, where would you go?"

I have no proof, but I was sure that I paled at the question. I'm still not sure whether He answered that question or I did, but the answer was obvious: Because I was damned, I would go to Hell. This is true because the Bible says, "For the wages of sin is death." The Lord went on to tell me that because He has so much love for each one of us, He has given us the freedom to choose where we will spend eternity. With Him, He was offering me everlasting life, love that knows no limits, and someone who sticks closer to you than a brother, no matter what you've done. Without Him, hell was my destination—pain, sorrow, and torment such as I had never known, for all eternity.

As the Lord spoke the words everlasting life, it was as though the words, starting with the letter e, proceeded from the hood of the Blazer out into the sky for as far as I could see.

Suddenly, I realized I was back in control of my vehicle, but during the interlude I'd traveled the entire thirty-five miles and was now close to home. Before I could even begin to contemplate what had just happened, I heard another voice.

"Sam," this new voice said. "You haven't been talking to the Lord. He's too big and too busy for you. It was just your imagination, Sam. Just your imagination."

Now, totally confused, I said in a big loud voice of my own, "God, I'm not sure, but I think I was talking to You. If I was, prove to me beyond a shadow of a doubt that I was, in fact, hearing from You."

Without knowing it, I had laid a fleece before God, and His answer was not long in coming.

About two weeks later, I had an opportunity to drop Stan off at his house on my way home from work. For the last two weeks, I had not mentioned my experience to anyone, so Stan knew nothing about it. I had to go to Big Springs on business the next day, so I mentioned to Stan that I wanted to him to go with me. To my amazement, he refused to go. I pressured him until he revealed to me the reason for his decision.

"Remember the last trip we took to Big Springs?" he asked. "Sam, that was the strangest trip I have ever taken in my whole life."

"Why?" I asked.

"Well," he said, "the trip to Big Springs was okay, but after we picked up your Blazer and headed out of town, things got very strange. I was following you, of course, and about five miles outside of Big Springs, it began to happen. Did you see the sky?"

"No, not particularly," I said.

"The sky was clear blue," he said. "All of a sudden, out of the northeast, three clouds appeared. They flew directly over us and stopped. Didn't you see them?"

"No, I didn't," I said.

"Those three clouds looked like three angels, and they stayed directly over us the whole way home."

When Stan told me that, I almost fell out of the car. There it was. God had used a friend, one who was as far away from Him as I was, to confirm to me that my encounter with Him two weeks earlier had been for real. I had all of the proof I needed to turn my life over to the Lord. However, I still rebelled. Fortunately for me, the story doesn't end there.

Within a year and a half, I had disposed of the business and was now living in Arizona. I had to return to Texas on business, and my wife, Donna, and I started out late one evening. Before long, she was sound asleep while I drove. Around one in the morning, I had my second encounter with the Lord.

As I drove along the interstate, the strange sensation of holding onto the wheel but not having control of the car occurred. The front of the vehicle and the road seemed to be in a tunnel surrounded by a cloud. No sooner did I realize what was happening than the same powerful, gentle, loving, and sweet voice of the Lord spoke to me again.

"Sam, how long are you going to wait?" He asked. "Time is so short, and there is so much work to do. Sam, now is the time."

Like I had done so often in the business world, I had put this decision "on my desk" and would get to it when I thought it was the opportune time. As I inhaled, the Lord brought a new meaning to word now. He explained that now meant with this very breath. I was expected to make my decision before I let my breath out.

With all of this before me, I still seemed to hang in my decision. In that moment, I looked heavenward and saw a sight I shall never forget. The stars and sky seemed to roll open like a scroll. I saw the angels of the Lord blow their trumpets, and I watched as God came to claim his own. I saw two workers in a field off to my right, and as I stared intently, one of them rose toward Heaven as he went to meet the Lord. The other, however, stayed behind.

As if that didn't have enough impact on me, the Lord brought it right to home for me. I saw myself riding in the car with Donna, who had been praying for me for years, and as we rode, the Lord called her and I saw her begin to rise through the roof of the car— going to meet the Lord in the air! I, on the other hand, was staying right where I was.

At that point I cried, "Wait a minute! I didn't want that. I was not ready for that!"

I asked the Lord to forgive me of my sins, to come into my heart, and to make me a new creature. That's exactly what He did. I was born again!

I woke Donna up and told her what had happened. At first, she didn't believe me, so I had to go through the whole story for her. My decision had been made to accept Jesus Christ as my Lord and Savior, and when I did, all of my sins were forgiven and my name, as the Bible says, was written down in God's book of the living, where I shall dwell with Him for all eternity.

Praise the Lord!

The story you have read is a true one. It really did happen to me. I didn't write this to impress anyone; I've written it for your benefit. I don't need real proof that there's a God of the universe, for I know without a shadow of a doubt that He exists. I also know there's a Heaven and a hell, where, due to our own choosing, we will spend eternity. You see, in His great love, God has given us the freedom to choose. He will not force anything upon us, not even Heaven. By ignoring the decision, you automatically choose hell, for we are all destined there from birth. To save us from the fiery depths, God sent His son, Jesus Christ to die on the cross for our sins. All you need to do is sincerely ask Him to forgive your sins, come into your heart, and make you a new person. If you make this decision, as I did, He will forgive you regardless of what you've done in life.

My friend, right now let me ask you:

Are you happy with your life?

Would you like to have someone you can go to that will help you with any tough decisions?

If you were to die today, or Jesus where to come today, where would you spend eternity? Heaven or hell?

Are you ready?

I trust you've already made the right decision. If you haven't, don't play games with your future, for it's far too important. Today, right now, with this very breath, as I did, ask Jesus to forgive you of your sins, to come into your heart and make you a new creature. He will. It's that simple!

ABOUT THE AUTHOR SAMUEL RADOBENKO

- As a Sunday School Teacher and Guest Speaker Samuel (Sam) Radobenko first came on the scene in the early "90's" with his teaching series Signs of the Times called "Decade of Destiny".

- After serving in the military as a Platoon Sergeant for Six Years, Sam was appointed to serve as a Chaplain to a Fire Department, where he served for Twelve Years.

- He resides in Mesa, Arizona, with his wife Donna of Fifty years. He is a family man. They have two children, one son, Sammy, and one daughter, Rachel. Sam met her for the first time during one of his journeys to heaven.

- He enjoys spending time with his family, Antique and older Muscle Cars, reading and learning through research.

- You may contact Sam on line at visionraider@yahoo.com or by mail at 2753 E. Broadway, S-101/133, Mesa, Arizona 85204

CPSIA information can be obtained
at www.ICGtesting.com
Printed in the USA
LVHW022245300520
656910LV00004B/307